Political Romanticism

Studies in Contemporary German Social Thought
Thomas McCarthy, General Editor

Political Romanticism

Carl Schmitt

translated by Guy Oakes

The MIT Press, Cambridge, Massachusetts, and London, England

First MIT Press paperback edition, 1991

This translation © 1986 by the Massachusetts Institute of Technology

This book was originally published as *Politische Romantik*, © 1919, 1925 by Duncker & Humblot, Berlin.

This book was set in Baskerville by DEKR.

Library of Congress Cataloging-in-Publication Data

Schmitt, Carl, 1888–
  Political romanticism.

  Translation of: Politische Romantik.
  Bibliography: p.
  Includes index.
  1. Political science—Europe—History—18th century.
2. Romanticism. I. Title.
JA84.E9S3313 1986   320.5'094   86-10252
ISBN 978-0-262-19252-1 (hc. : alk. paper) — 978-0-262-69142-0 (pb. : alk. paper)

Contents

Contents

Translator's Introduction

The *j'accuse* mode of intellectuality: Schmitt and the polemical style of thought

By the summer of 1945, Carl Schmitt had witnessed the civil war of 1918 and the collapse of the Wilhelmian Reich, the rise, vicissitudes, and fall of the Weimar Republic, the hazards of public life in the Third Reich, the Allied bombings of Berlin, and the catastrophic end of the Second World War. Along with an acute instinct for survival, he had also demonstrated a remarkable capacity for accommodation. As a professor at Bonn (1922–1928), Schmitt was an active supporter of political Catholicism and the policies of Heinrich Brüning, the leader of the Catholic Center party. In addition, many of his articles on political matters during this period appeared in the Catholic press.[1] Throughout the constitutional crises of the Weimar Republic, Schmitt was the most articulate advocate of discretionary presidential power that would make it possible to defend the Republic under emergency conditions. He also consistently supported a broad interpretation of Article 48 of the Weimar Constitution, which granted the Reich president the authority to suspend basic constitutional rights and take extraordinary measures in order to eliminate threats to public order.[2] With Schmitt's move to Berlin in 1928, his constitutional interpretations acquired more influence. He became a protégé of Johannes Popitz, a Prussian aristocrat and high civil servant, and he managed to establish himself as an informal adviser to General Kurt von Schleicher, a Hindenburg confidant and an influential power broker in Berlin. Finally, Schmitt was eventually engaged as a constitutional adviser to the Hindenburg government under the chancellorship of Heinrich Brüning. From this position, he was able to supply the arguments that formed the legal basis of the presidential system that governed the Republic by means of extraparliamentary decrees during the repeated electoral crises of the period 1930–1932.

By 1932, Schmitt's public position on the National Socialists was clear. The ultimate objective of the Nazi party was to destroy the Weimar Constitution and its political order. The government, which was obligated to uphold the Constitution, could not consistently maintain a dispassionate and neutral stance vis-à-vis such a party. This meant that the National Socialists, along with the Communists, had to be denied the "equal chance" to compete for political power that was guaranteed constitutional parties. In Schmitt's view, a decision to place the National Socialists on the same legal footing with parties committed to the Weimar Constitution would amount to a reductio ad absurdum of the Constitution itself. In his essay *Legalität und Legitimität,* written during the months immediately preceding the general elections of July 1932, Schmitt argued that it would be ridiculous to suppose that the Constitution includes a legal means of nullifying its own legality, and even more absurd to suppose that it provides a method for authorizing the destruction of the system of order instituted by the Constitution itself.[3] In the context of the political struggles of that year, it did not require a prodigal imagination to read this argument as an admonition against the current electoral strategy of the Nazi party leadership and its attempt to destroy the Constitution by gaining control of the state through legal means. Schmitt made his position on the National Socialists even more unequivocal in a newspaper article published less than two weeks before the general elections. It was called "The Abuse of Legality."

Whoever provides the National Socialists with the majority on July 31 — even though he is not a National Socialist and regards this party only as the lesser evil — acts *foolishly.* he gives this movement — which is ideologically oriented and politically still quite immature — the *possibility* of changing the Constitution, setting up a state ecclesiastical authority, dissolving the trade unions, and so on. He delivers Germany completely into the hands of this group.[4]

In spite of his support for the Republic, his criticism of the Nazis, and his ties to prominent Jews, in both academia and the government,[5] Schmitt managed to execute a brilliant and astonishingly smooth transition from Weimar to the Third Reich. Although he did not join the party until May 1933, his collaboration with the National Socialist government began less than three months after Hitler's appointment as chancellor, when Schmitt was asked to assist in drafting legislation to legalize the Nazi reorganization and control of state governments. Within a short time, Schmitt was able to secure the patronage of Goering and Hans Frank. Appointment to a number of party posts and party-influenced offices followed, making Schmitt one of the most visible academic sympathizers and intellectual ornaments of the new order. Although General von Schleicher was a victim of the purges of 1934, Schmitt himself was left untouched, and within a month of the so-called Night of the Long Knives, he had an article in print defending the legality of Hitler's actions.[6] In 1936, Schmitt's enemies in both academic and party bureaucracies engineered a Gestapo investigation into his Weimar past and the opportunism of his rapprochement with the Nazis. As a result of this inquiry, Schmitt was stripped of his government and party appointments, but he escaped with his life and his academic career intact. He was also able to survive the aftermath of the twentieth of July conspiracy to assassinate Hitler, the failure of which resulted in the execution of his political ally Johannes Popitz. And in spite of the impressive record he had compiled as a supporter of the Third Reich, Schmitt even managed to escape the complicated legal machinery constructed by the Allied War Crimes Tribunal at Nuremberg. Schmitt had defended the legality of the National Socialist regime, vindicated Hitler's status as the supreme judge and legislator of the German nation, and elaborated a Monroe Doctrine for Europe that would legitimize the new pan-European German empire.[7] Yet after more than a year in internment camps and a period of interrogation at Nuremberg, no indictment was brought against Schmitt, and he was allowed to retire to the comparative tranquillity of his home town in the rural Sauerland.

Writing in an apparently introspective mood of self-examination in the summer of 1945, Schmitt describes himself as a contemplative spirit, not inclined to take the intellectual offensive and, for that matter, not disposed to the counterattack either.

> But I am also weak at defense. I have too little practical interest in myself and too much theoretical interest in the ideas of my opponents, even when they come forward as accusers. I am too curious about the intellectual presuppositions of every reproach, every accusation, and every accuser. This is why I am no good either as a defendant or as an accuser. And yet I always prefer to be the defendant rather than the accuser. The *j'accuse* types may have their role to play on the world stage. For me, the prosecutorial role is even more uncomfortable than the inquisitorial.[8]

Nothing, of course, could be further from the truth. Schmitt was the consummate "prosecutorial" thinker, and all his major works were developed as attempts to destroy positions he rejected. Schmitt's scholarly career began with an ambitious polemic against the dominant positivist jurisprudence of his time, especially its theory of judicial interpretation and decision making[9] and its conception of the legitimacy of state power.[10] Immediately after the collapse of the Wilhelmian Reich, Schmitt launched an attack on the neo-Kantian interpretation of the nature and limits of legal authority and its theory of the normative basis of the state.[11] Even his most ambitious scholarly work of the Weimar period — the *Verfassungslehre* (Constitutional theory) — was in part a sustained assault on the formalistic analysis of the Constitution favored by neo-Kantian jurisprudence, and an attempt to refute the conception of the Constitution as ultimately grounded in basic norms or axioms.[12] Schmitt's three most widely discussed books were also clearly polemical in their intent. His analysis of parliamentary democracy was a critique of the political philosophy of liberalism and the institution of parliament that questioned their viability in the modern democratic order.[13] The tract *The Concept of the Political* defended a conception of politics as determined by unconditional conflicts that entail the necessity of drawing an absolute distinction between friend and enemy. It attacked the liberal conception of politics as compromise and discussion and the liberal theory of the relationship between the state and the politically neutral spheres of culture, such as religion, the economy, and the family.[14] In *Legalität und Legitimität*, Schmitt's target was a purely formal, value-neutral, and procedural jurisprudence that ignores the basic substantive values to which the Constitution is committed. In fact, the very book in which Schmitt took such pains to deny the polemical cast of his thought was also a polemic, an apologia for the life of a thinker who made the intellectual and moral sacrifices that were essential to success in the new german order, accommodations that ended in a bizarre internal exile that was characteristic of many fractured and compromised careers during the Third Reich.[15]

Political Romanticism is the most contentious of all Schmitt's books, the work in which he embraces the *j'accuse* role with an unqualified enthusiasm. Beginning with a critique of the received theory of romanticism, in which the romantic is defined by reference to certain objects of emotional attachment, Schmitt moves on to attack the fundamental principles of the romantic movement, concentrating especially on the metaphysical basis of romanticism and its aestheticization of all spheres of culture. The major arguments of the book are reserved for Schmitt's assault on political romanticism and its "poeticization" of political conflicts. This critique includes a more general attack on the European bourgeoisie as the class that embraced romanticism and thereby depoliticized the liberal social order by transforming political debate into an endless conversation in which the pursuit of amusement and self-indulgence render genuine political decisions impossible. Finally, Schmitt's own political sympathies lie with Edmund Burke, Joseph de Maistre, and Louis Bonald, with the political philosophy of conservatism, the post-Napoleonic restoration, and — at least until the mid-1920s — with political Catholicism.

As an enemy of romanticism, therefore, he must in particular refute the view that political romanticism is intrinsically linked with conservatism, the restoration, or Catholicism, and dispose of conventional interpretations of Burke, Bonald, and de Maistre as advocates of political romanticism.

The romantic attitude

Schmitt's analysis of the romantic movement begins with a critique of three generally accepted conceptions of romanticism. First, romanticism cannot be ostensively defined by a collection of objects or artifacts that are said to be romantic because of certain distinctive properties they have in common. Thus it cannot be said that mountainous landscapes, primitive societies, architectural ruins, mysticism, lyric poetry, love songs, or the Middle Ages are intrinsically romantic. Second, romanticism cannot be defined by reference to a purely psychological state. Thus romanticism cannot be understood as emotionality, innocence, a love of adventure, or a flight into the remote, the exotic, or the alien. Finally, it is also necessary to reject a dichotomous conception of romanticism that represents it as the polar antithesis of classicism or rationalism. There are two reasons why such a dichotomous conception is mistaken. First, these dichotomies are not exhaustive. From the fact that an artifact is not a product of classicism or rationalism, it does not follow that it falls within the domain of the romantic. For example, Schmitt argues that Roman Catholicism is mistakenly linked with romanticism because it is not a product of rationalism, and the modern historical consciousness is fallaciously attributed to romanticism because its genesis lies in a critique of eighteenth-century rationalism. Second, what qualifies as classicism or rationalism is historically variable. If classicism is understood as the culture of classical antiquity, then its historical antithesis is the Christian culture of the Middle Ages. But classicism may also be identified with the aesthetic principles dominant in the French high culture of the seventeenth century, in which case its antithesis is the German Sturm und Drang of the late eighteenth century. Schmitt concludes that it is preposterous to suppose that romanticism can be defined in terms of properties that the medieval culture of Christianity and the German literary culture of the late eighteenth century have in common.

According to Schmitt, these views of romanticism are committed to a naive realism that assumes that certain objects or artifacts are inherently romantic, independent of how they are conceived and experienced. In opposition to this assumption, Schmitt contends that an adequate analysis of romanticism must begin with a characteristic attitude and its posture toward the world. Like any other cultural movement, the romantic movement rests on a distinctive set of commitments and the idea of an ultimate axiom or a final authority, the basic metaphysical principle on which these commitments rest. In the language of German philosophical idealism that Schmitt often favors, romanticism is not defined realistically, by reference to a certain collection of objects, but rather transcendentally, in terms of the romantic subject or person: a specific type of human being and its characteristic mode of existence. Schmitt also insists that the way to understand a metaphysical position is not to analyze it in the abstract, but rather to explore the concrete situations and circumstances of life in which its commitments are exhibited. Suppose we take this suggestion seriously.

A young man named Johannes finds himself strolling the streets of Copenhagen on an early April evening. By chance he notices an innocent-looking young girl who strikes his fancy. He follows her to a shop, where he manages to observe her without being detected. Seeing that she does not wear a wedding band, he hears that she is about to give her address to a clerk but takes care not to listen, ensuring that he does not deprive himself of a future agreeable surprise. Instead he withdraws, savoring the expectation of another chance meeting in unexpected circumstances. This duly happens when he encounters her on another aimless stroll, whereupon he manages to discover both her name (Cordelia) and residence. He cleverly arranges an introduction, which is followed by furtive and carefully calculated observations that disclose a quiet, modest, sensitive girl, possessed of great passion and imagination that seem to have remain untapped. In other words, here is an object worthy of a seduction, which Johannes plans with the consummate care of the master artist who works in that most recalcitrant and unpredictable of media, the interplay of human emotions.

His plan is complex, elegant, and ironical. First, he will find an object for her emotions, not by immediately interesting her in himself, but rather by providing her with an appropriate suitor: a respectable and attractive young man, but someone who will prove incapable of plumbing the depths of her feelings. Pursuing this strategy, Johannes choreographs an adolescent infatuation between Cordelia and the hapless Edvard, whose deficiencies give her both a distaste for love and a desire to transcend her own limitations. This experience of the disparity between the suitor's banality and her own emotional possibilities also gives Cordelia a more precise sense of what a proper object of her desires should be. Ultimately, the suitor will bore her, and she will despair of the possibility of erotic love, a despair that — given the appropriate occasion — Johannes will be able to dissolve. This will make Cordelia all the more interesting. Not only will he enjoy the contemplation of her nascent passion, the inadequacy of its satisfaction, and her premature despair. He will also be able to observe her spontaneous delight in discovering the differences between himself and the suitor as potential lovers. Thus his plan is to form a series of purely aesthetic contrasts that will serve as objects for his own contemplative pleasure.

Johannes carries out this plan. Cordelia is first flattered and then bored by the suitor he has provided for her. At that point, she begins to find Johannes himself intriguing and discovers that she is excited by his detachment, intellectuality, and apparent inaccessibility — unaware, of course, that Johannes is playing with the cultivation of her emotions. After he has succeeded in fascinating Cordelia, Johannes plants a rumor that he is in love with a young girl, intending that this rumor will find its way to Cordelia and pique her curiosity. This duly happens, and when Johannes judges that the emotional circumstances are right, he proposes to Cordelia that they become engaged. The proposal is, of course, ironically rather than seriously intended. Exploiting the ambivalent status and the unresolved possibilities inherent in the engagement, he aims to become the object of Cordelia's love, but only so that he can enjoy the pleasures of contemplating himself in this state. In other words, Johannes does not intend to assume any responsibilities. He acts only in the realm of fantasy. He makes no commitments that would bind him to the norms of mundane reality and its expectations. This is why his strategy is to translate the engagement from a practical act subject to the demands of morality into an imaginative incident governed by considerations that are exclusively aesthetic. As a result, Cordelia will experience this aestheticized engagement, not as something she does, but as something that happens to her, as an event or an episode rather than an action.

The aesthetic principles that govern Johannes's life require that any relationship be terminated before boredom and routine set in. Otherwise the possibility of surprise and the enjoyment of unexpected moods would be destroyed. Therefore, once the aesthetic possibilities of the engagement have been exhausted, Johannes will make sure that it is swiftly dissolved. Further, it must be Cordelia herself who breaks the engagement, and she must do this willingly, even willfully, in the belief that she can realize her desires only by escaping the confines of a conventional erotic relationship. This will, of course, absolve Johannes of any responsibility for the affair. Thus Johannes's tactic is to develop in Cordelia a passion for him that becomes so unconditional that she will regard the engagement as a tiresome compromise and a hindrance to true love. Once in the grip of this higher passion, Cordelia will transcend the practical expectations of the engagement. At that point, she will free herself from the bonds of moral limitations because she has learned how to aestheticize her own life and play freely with it. In other words, she will break the engagement in order to surrender herself to a passion that has been evoked, shaped, and directed by Johannes. And at that point, of course, the seduction of Cordelia is complete.

Johannes worships at the altar of the goddess of chance. Caprice provides the opportunities he needs to discover a girl worth seducing. For Johannes, reality has no inherent structure or meaning. It is significant only insofar as it provides occasions on which he can exercise his aesthetic imagination. These occasions are pure contingencies that are not connected in any orderly or coherent way. Other persons as well are nothing more than raw material on which the artist in human relationships works. Johannes makes Cordelia into an aesthetic artifact, the embodiment of an idea that is a product of his fancy. The realization of this idea, however, depends upon the development of her own self-consciousness and her capacity to experience herself as the object he imagines her to be. As he cultivates Cordelia's emotional life, Johannes is able to enjoy increasingly sophisticated pleasures. There are the pleasures of the eye: his enjoyment of Cordelia's physical presence and company, although in view of the seducer's disposition to intellectualize the sensual and transform it into an object of refined contemplation, this can hardly be regarded as a simple sensuous delight. There are also the pleasures Johannes takes in observing Cordelia's enjoyment of her own ambivalent and intoxicating situation, a pleasure that stems from his contemplation of the product of his ingenuity. There is the satisfaction he finds in reflecting that he has formed her passion in the way that an artist creates a work of art, a pleasure of the artistic imagination. There is the satisfaction that results from the knowledge that, in experiencing these delights, he risks nothing, no potentially painful and embarrassing moral consequences — the pleasures of the moral nihilist. Finally, there is the delight he takes in observing himself enjoying the artifact he has created — a narcissistic pleasure of self-contemplation.

In transforming his own life into a work of art and thereby escaping the tedium of the everyday world, Johannes must refuse to subject himself to the requirements of ethical principles. He must remain aloof from the exigencies of moral commitments and the responsibilities that arise from assuming obligations. Johannes conceives the moral regulation of life as a grim and spiritually numbing discipline, a predetermined pattern mapped out on a grid of ethical routines. Such a moral routinization of existence would destroy the caprice, the irony, and the imaginative play essential to the life of the aesthete and eroticist who is committed to the task of living poetically.

This young man, the protagonist of Kierkegaard's *Diary of a Seducer,* is a romantic.[16]

According to Schmitt, romanticism began as an aesthetic movement with two chief tendencies. It repudiated the aesthetic principles of the past, but without replacing them with new principles that would articulate its own distinctive conception of style and form. And it absolutized art and thereby aestheticized every sphere of culture: religion, science, ethics, politics, and erotics. In destroying aesthetic forms, it rendered all other forms problematic. The result was the subjectification of life, produced by the general collapse of objective standards, and the privatization of experience. Schmitt argues that in order to place romanticism in modern intellectual history, it is essential to grasp the main consequence of the development of metaphysics during the last three centuries: the displacement of a transcendent God as the basic metaphysical principle. To understand this development, it is necessary to begin with the philosophy of Descartes, which is dominated by the absolute dichotomies of mind and body, subject and object, the ego and the world. Schmitt traces romanticism to the tradition of philosophical occasionalism as systematized in the thought of Malebranche and his response to the difficulties posed by Descartes's metaphysical dualism. In the occasionalist resolution of the Cartesian problem of the relation between mind and body, God becomes the cause of both mental and physical events and also of the interactions between them. With regard to a theory of the person and a philosophical account of human action, this means that it is not the human being who acts, but rather God, for whom the person is only an occasion. The world itself becomes nothing more than contingent material for the action of God, the true reality. In Schmitt's account of the philosophical premises of romanticism, the romantic movement retains the basic metaphysical attitude of traditional philosophical occasionalism, but abandons its ultimate principle.

The collapse of the traditional idea of God in the eighteenth century raised the question of what could take its place as the fundamental metaphysical principle. At the end of the eighteenth century, two new ontological pretenders made a claim to this status: humanity or the "revolutionary god," variously conceived as the people, the general will, the public, or society; and the "conservative god," conceived as historically unique cultures, traditions, and nations that restored what society had revolutionized. The posture of romanticism in relation to these two new "demiurges" of modern thought may be characterized in this way: It grounds them both in the subjective imagination, thereby transforming their import and their values. God is replaced by the emancipated, private individual of the bourgeois social order. The romantic ego now becomes the final metaphysical authority. In this sense, the romantic movement represents both a process of secularization and a process of subjectification and privatization. Schmitt concludes that romanticism may be understood as subjectified occasionalism. The world becomes nothing more than an occasion for the free play of the individual imagination. Schmitt's discussion of the essential features of romanticism may be reconstructed by differentiating three doctrines.

Ontological aestheticism

The romantic attitude is defined by caprice, the denial of a binding and predictable causality. This entails the negation of all consistency, both nomological and normative. In the metaphysics of romanticism, the world has no independent or intrinsic reality. Even an event of world-historical importance such as the French Revolution or the First World War has no inherent ontological significance. This means that nothing can be said to exist because of its own substantive qualities, for example, the properties that can be ascribed to it by virtue of its historical, political, or moral status. Romanticism entails that there are no such properties. An item exists only as an object of an aesthetic interest, and the world is constituted by the essentially capricious states of the individual aesthetic imagination. The content of subjective emotional life determines what is real. This means that reality can be ascribed to an item only insofar as it becomes an occasion for an emotional experience, regardless of whether this emotion is an innocuous mood, a shattering impression, or a great flash of insight. In the ontology of Johannes the Seducer, for example, Cordelia exists only as a product of his aesthetic fancy. This position can be called ontological aestheticism. Because the world is constituted by the subjective imagination, it follows that regardless of what seems to occupy the individual, he is really concerned only with himself. Thus it can be said that romanticism is committed to a metaphysical narcissism: The limits of my experience and the limits of what exists are ultimately the limits of the self in which I am aesthetically interested. The experience of Johannes also makes this point clear. Regardless of whether he is arranging an appointment, making polite conversation, drafting a letter, or planning an erotic conquest, the object of his interest is always the same: himself and the perfection of his life as a work of art. Romanticism transforms the world but, as the experience of Johannes shows, only in appearance, only in the imaginative domain of play and sensibility.

Irony

Romanticism is philosophically revolutionary because it destroys the primacy of reality and replaces it with the primacy of unlimited possibilities. The romantic interest in the remote, the exotic, the alien, and the erotic — for example, Johannes's interest in young women — does not ascribe any intrinsic significance to these phenomena. On the contrary, the romanticized object is significant only as a way of devaluating contemporary reality and escaping the limitations of the here and now. The romantic plays off possible worlds against one another, with the result that the finite world of mundane existence is paralyzed.[17] This does not mean that romanticism denies the reality of routine existence and everyday life. Such a denial would presuppose another objective possibility on the basis of which this denial is made. The acknowledgment of an alternative ontological criterion would recognize the possibility of an objective world that exists independent of its interest for the aesthetic imagination. The admission of such a possibility would contradict the doctrine of ontological aestheticism. This is the ultimate reason why Johannes cannot allow moral considerations to play any role in his stratagems. To do so would acknowledge a world governed by objective moral norms, "objective" in the sense that their content and validity are independent of the romantic ego. Thus Johannes cannot admit the legitimacy of moral norms — or any other objectively binding principles, including the ontological principles that would nullify the reality of everyday life — without ceasing to be a romantic. Reality is suspended by the romantic game, which plays it off against a fantasized or imagined reality. The romantic suspends the mundane world, not by actually escaping into another world, but by allowing himself to be gripped by his imagination. Reality is not nullified by a flight into the past, the exotic, or the erotic. It is instead neutralized by dreamlike fantasies of antiquity, adventure, and love. The romanticized object is of interest only insofar as it can serve as an occasional impulse, another first move in a *Phantasiespiel*, a play of fantasy or a game of the imagination in which reality is aestheticized in the interest of achieving an appropriate mood. Since the question of what can serve as an impulse for a mood is entirely capricious, no intrinsic significance is ascribed to the fantasized reality. This *Phantasiespiel* is the basis of romantic irony.[18] The free play of the imagination is safeguarded by a process of ontological relativization and a refusal to recognize any principle outside its own sphere. Thus it admits no limitations on its activity except its own immanent aesthetic limitations.

Schmitt notes that romantic irony is opposed to self-irony. The object of romantic irony is not the romantic himself, but rather the world. Self-irony objectifies the subject or the self. As a result, the self becomes an object for another subject and its standards. The recognition of these standards, however, would compromise the supremacy of the aesthetic imagination. In other words, self-irony would destroy the sovereignty of the romantic ego, which would also destroy romanticism itself. As the case of Kierkegaard's seducer demonstrates, ultimately the only thing the romantic takes seriously is his own aesthetic consciousness, and that is why he cannot treat himself as an object of romantic play.

Poeticization

The result of romantic irony is a "poeticization" of the world. In the phrase of Novalis, the world is of interest only insofar as it provides material for the beginning of an endless novel or, in Friedrich Schlegel's metaphor, themes for an endless conversation. Poeticization can be represented as the transformation of all spheres of culture into aesthetics. Science, religion, politics, and ethics are reduced to the domain of affect. Both instrumentally productive activity and morally responsible conduct are devaluated in favor of "poeticizing." Theory and practice are reduced to aesthetic contemplation, and theoretical contradictions and practical conflicts are reduced to aesthetic contrasts that provoke pleasurable and elevating experiences. The process of poeticization begins when the romantic confronts a conflict in the real world. He does not attempt to resolve this conflict. He does not even recognize it as a substantive conflict between real alternatives. On the contrary, he regards it as a fortunate occasion for the evocation of an emotionally satisfying mood, an aesthetic opportunity. In order to stimulate this mood, he translates the conflict into a state of emotional discord. A real opposition is "paraphrased" as an emotive dissonance. Reality is transposed into the aesthetic language of the music of the emotions. This paraphrase is then subjected to the creative play of the imagination, with the result that the dissonance is reconciled. This is the process of romantic sublimation. Poeticization does not resolve the conflict, but rather suspends it by incorporating the antithetical factors into a higher harmony.

The seducer's relationship with Cordelia is a good example of poeticization. Johannes is not unaware of the moral problems posed by his attempt to deceive an innocent young girl in order to satisfy his own whims. How does he confront these problems? He does not try to resolve them. He does not even recognize them as moral issues. For Johannes, Cordelia is not a person to whom he has moral obligations, but rather a happy occasion for a new emotional experience or, at the very least, an opportunity for avoiding boredom. A moral relationship between two persons is translated into the aesthetic relationship between the artist and his material. The ethical demands of conscience are transposed into the requirements of the aesthetic consciousness. Boredom takes the place of the morally reprehensible, and contemplative delight replaces what is morally responsible. This does not mean that Johannes refuses to countenance any limitations on his conduct or that he regards all possibilities as permissible in the poeticization of life. He will not allow himself to be consumed by passion. This would destroy the "cool" disposition that is essential to the enjoyment of a young girl. If he succumbs to his own feelings and permits himself to be emotionally overwhelmed, the delights of contemplation will be impossible. He also refuses to play upon Cordelia's passions. He does not want to achieve a swift conquest by waging an emotional blitzkrieg that would leave her helpless. That would be "aesthetically wrong." But these limitations are not a consequence of moral considerations. They are imposed by the aesthetic imperatives of the romantic attitude. The reduction of the moral conflict between the cunning seducer and his innocent victim to the aesthetics of the relationship between the artist and his material does not resolve this conflict. It rather paraphrases the conflict or transposes it into a contest between the ingenuity of the artist and the resistance of his medium. In this contest, Johannes allows his imagination free play within the limits of what is aesthetically permissible and emotionally necessary. The result is a precious moment, a piquant mood that becomes even richer in inner emotion when Johannes contemplates his own enjoyment of it.

The romantic attitude, therefore, is defined by reference to three principles. Ontological aestheticism: The world is constituted by the emotional states of the subjective imagination. Irony: The real world of routine existence is suspended and relativized by means of a fantasized world. Poeticization: The substantive conflicts of the real world are aesthetically paraphrased and transposed into a higher, emotionally satisfying harmony.[19]

Political romanticism

Schmitt traces the prehistory of political romanticism by examining its relationship to revolutionary and reactionary tendencies in modern European history. Paradoxically, both the most enthusiastic partisans of the French Revolution and its most embittered enemies were numbered among the romantics. And during the movement for German national unity at the beginning of the nineteenth century, both revolutionaries and reactionaries counted themselves as romantics. According to Schmitt, the use of the concept to designate diametrically opposed political positions is less paradoxical than it seems. The situation results from the occasionalist character of political romanticism: its capricious quality and its lack of commitment to any substantive political position. In light of this consideration, received scholarly opinion is mistaken in the supposition that there is anything distinctively conservative, traditional, legitimist, or reactionary about romanticism. The restoration is no more or less intrinsically romantic than the Revolution, and a hero of the Revolution such as Danton is just as much a potential object of romantic interest as a legitimate monarch such as Frederick the Great.

Before moving to a systematic analysis of political romanticism, Schmitt proposes to clarify the phenomenon in a preliminary way by examining what he calls the praxis of political romanticism. This is undertaken by documenting the way political romanticism was expressed in the careers of two German literati and pseudopolitical figures, Friedrich Schlegel (1772–1823) and Adam Müller (1779–1829). The purpose of this sketch is to illustrate Schmitt's thesis that political romanticism is not a coherent doctrine with an internally consistent core of central ideas. On the contrary, the romantic movement was politically inconsequential and impotent. The political activity of early romantics such as Friedrich Schlegel and Adam Müller was characterized by extreme vacillation and indecision, the absence of any unequivocal principles or definitive commitments, an indifference to the real substance of political issues, and an inclination to live off politics rather than for politics.

According to Schmitt, the variability of the political content of romanticism and the remarkable plasticity of the political romantics — their ability to accommodate themselves to the entire spectrum of political positions — are a consequence of the romantic reduction of politics to aesthetics. Because political romanticism poeticizes politics, political issues become nothing more than an occasion for the exercise of the aesthetic imagination. Political conflicts are translated into aesthetic contrasts, which are suspended in a higher unity achieved by the play of emotion. Schmitt claims that politics is ultimately concerned with the necessity of deciding between what is right and what is wrong, and between what is just and what is unjust. This means that politics depends upon two things: a decision made in a conflict over what is right and wrong; and what Schmitt calls a concept of what is right, a principle or a criterion of justice to which this decision is committed.[20]

In Schmitt's analysis of political romanticism, the poeticization of politics rests on a romantic theory of action. This theory is a consequence of the three doctrines that define the romantic attitude. The romantic acts in such a way that his imagination can be acted upon or affected. He acts insofar as he is moved. Thus an action is not a performance or something one does, but rather an affect or a mood, something one feels. The product of an action is not a result that can be evaluated according to moral standards, but rather an emotional experience that can be judged only in aesthetic and emotive terms. As the Kierkegaardian seducer realized, the romantic is amoral in the sense that he does not concern himself with moral problems. He does not acknowledge any moral position because he does not make moral commitments. To do so would amount to the recognition of norms that hold independently of his own emotional experience, and such an admission would be inconsistent with the romantic attitude. Philosophically, it can be said that the romantic theory of action is committed to an emotive ethics. Something is good when it feels good, bad when it feels bad. In the romantic ethic, therefore, an action is good or bad independent of both its intentions and its practical consequences. The moral qualities of an action depend exclusively upon whether it expresses or evokes certain emotional states. And psychologically, it can be said that the romantic theory of action is committed to an ethic of passivity, quietism, or indifference. One acts only in the sense that one feels, experiences, or suffers emotional states.

Schmitt notes that the favorite occupation of the political romantic is criticism. Discussion or conversation is the vehicle by which the romantic poeticizes politics. It is the medium in which the romantic imagination plays with political values, sublimating them as points of view or feelings, and suspending the opposition between them in an emotionally satisfying inner synthesis that transcends the world of real political conflict. As a result, political issues become an occasion for something that is not political: the creative play of the *Wortspiel*, the play with words, which has as its purpose the delight taken in the game itself. In this way, political discourse is transposed into a discussion that is governed by aesthetic and emotive considerations. Politics becomes an aesthetically satisfying conversation, a source of escape, amusement, or even emotional elevation.

In the endless conversation of political romanticism, no political decision is ever made. No commitment is undertaken, no responsibility is assumed, and nothing in political reality is changed. Because politics has become "lyrical," nothing gets done. Points of view are expressed, but not with a view to making choices that would actually produce practical results. Conversation is instead a vehicle for the aesthetic satisfaction of the political actor, who is conceived as an autoerotic raconteur, an adept and devotee of a higher chatter that serves as a means of generating the appropriate feelings. The conversation of the political romantic must be endless because its termination would either resolve the political conflict or fix opposing conceptions of right and wrong in mutually irreconcilable positions. The claim that the conflict can be resolved implies a principle on the basis of which right and wrong can be distinguished. The claim that the conflict cannot be resolved implies a principle on the basis of which the resolution of the conflict can be shown to be impossible. In either case, the political romantic would be obliged to acknowledge a norm that is independent of the play of his imagination, which means that he would cease to be a romantic.

In the United States, recent history has produced a remarkable flourishing of political romanticism, especially in the period now called the sixties, the age of experience that was "more electrical than ethical."[21] Like Adam Müller and Friedrich Schlegel, the German romantics of the early nineteenth century whom Schmitt regards as the paradigmatic figures of political romanticism, the American political romantics of the 1960s were obsessively fascinated with themselves and compulsively devoted to self-disclosure and self-celebration. During this period, no one achieved the poeticization of the political more completely than the irrepressible Norman Mailer. In an era that made possible Leonard Bernstein's party for the Black Panthers, the reputation of Susan Sontag and Charles Reich as serious cultural critics, the status of Herbert Marcuse as the philosopher of an important social movement, and the prophetic calling of Timothy Leary, an era in which "the Woodstock generation" and "the denim revolution" could be regarded as significant political forces, and the exercise of taste in articles of mass consumption and conformity to certain fashions governing drug use, cosmetics, hair style, sexual conduct, and the ornamentation of the body could be treated as authentic political statements, this was no mean accomplishment.[22] Suppose we rejoin him in Washington, D.C., in October 1967. The occasion is the protest against American participation in the war in Vietnam. Some 35,000 people held a rally at the Lincoln Memorial and then crossed the Arlington Memorial Bridge to march to the Pentagon, where some were arrested for attempting to occupy the Department of Defense and disrupt its operations. Why is Norman Mailer in Washington, and what is he doing?

In fact, he doesn't seem to know. Apparently there were so many reasons and they were so equivocal that Mailer was unable to identify even one of them. The reasons, if indeed there were any, are transformed into conversational material for the self-congratulatory musings over breakfast at the Hay-Adams Hotel in the company of the poet Robert Lowell and the critic Dwight McDonald. They were an occasion for good feelings and an "unspoken happy confidence," and ultimately they provided the raw material for the book in which Mailer records his experience of the march and the impact this experience made on him: *The Armies of the Night: History as a Novel, the Novel as History.*[23] During the weekend of the march, Mailer translates a political issue about what American policy in South-

east Asia should be into an occasion for emotional satisfaction.
The march provides Mailer with an opportunity for intense
and highly self-conscious emotional reveries in which he becomes a spectator of his own moods. He contemplates his
contempt for the liberal academics participating in the march
and his ambivalent attitude toward Robert Lowell. He worries
about whether he has spoken well, frets over whether an audience of demonstrators received his remarks with more enthusiasm than they displayed for Lowell, wonders whether
Lowell liked his speech and — more important — liked him,
and focuses on the various stages of his drunkenness and han-
govers. After the accumulated excitement of his speech on the
eve of the march, the march itself, and his arrest, incarceration,
and release, Mailer, the "emotional connoisseur," pauses to
"steep the essences of this experience at his leisure," so that it
can be preserved as a part of the permanent collection in the
museum of his imagination.[24] In short, the march is a good
thing for Mailer because, in various ways, it makes him feel
good.

Ultimately, the march is an opportunity for Mailer to reaf-
firm and enjoy his own celebrity: the public exhibition of his
status as a prophet, seer, and "sexalogue." Nor on this score
does he leave much to chance, for a British television crew is
on the scene documenting Mailer's participation in these pro-
ceedings. At his speech in the Ambassador Theater, on the
march over the Arlington Memorial Bridge, during the mo-
ments of his arrest by a United States marshal at the Pentagon,
on the occasion of his release from jail, and at the conclusion
of his hearing, the comforting presence of the film crew is
there, accompanying him at close range, assuaging his loneli-
ness and recording his acts. But what are these acts? Mailer
does not try to resolve the conflicts over American foreign
policy that provided the occasion for the march. Nor does he
see the march, his experience, and the book in which he reflects
on his experience as a contribution to their resolution. Mailer
does not participate in any decisions on what should be done
about these issues. He makes no commitments and accepts no
responsibility for the march or its consequences. Indeed, as his
speech at the Ambassador Theater shows, he is not even pre-

pared to assume responsibility for his own conduct. Mailer's
acts are exercises of the imagination in which he plays with the
material of politics and history, material that serves as the
beginning of a "novel" in which he is both the artist and the
protagonist.

Throughout the weekend of the march, things happen to
Mailer. He is arrested, filmed, incarcerated, and released. But
his actions remain within the sphere of the emotive. He acts
only insofar as he feels. He stimulates his own sensibilities,
arousing himself by drinking and fantasizing, and he talks
about how he feels, heightening the contemplation of his feelings as objects of delight. In this regard, Mailer displays the
passivity of the political romantic, which Schmitt sees as a consequence of the poeticization of politics. Schmitt argues that
romantic passivity is exhibited in various ways: in the conception of man as a plaything or a tool of hidden forces; in a
mistrust of the artifices of the "political geometers" and an
aversion to political plans in general;[25] and in the obscure
feeling that the individual is a member of a higher organism
that is not subject to human agency. It is primarily expressed,
however, in a general indecisiveness and a disposition to escape
the either-or of ultimate value conflicts, both of which result
in the inability to make choices. Because moral and political
decisions appear as the imposition of an antiromantic tyranny,
the romantic attitude suspends practical judgments in the interest of preserving the spontaneity of sentiment. This is a
consequence of the radical transformation of praxis entailed
by the romantic theory of action: The moral and political faculties of willing, choosing, deciding, and acting are poeticized
as aesthetic faculties of feeling, emoting, and fantasizing. If
ethical conduct and political action are concerned with deciding
between alternative values and making commitments on the
basis of choices between these values, then it can be said that
romanticism either destroys the sphere of ethical and political
choice or sublimates it into an interplay of moods and sentiments. According to Schmitt, this means that romanticism is
incompatible with politics. Put another way, political romanticism is an incoherent concept: The romantic attitude makes
politics impossible because the poeticization of politics nullifies

the conditions under which choices between alternative conceptions of right and wrong, of justice and injustice, can be made.

The poeticization of politics seems to entail that political romanticism is apolitical. The romantic is impressionable, capricious, irresponsible, and passive. He is disposed to favor mere discussion, in the form of idle and amusing chatter, over action. As a result, he is incapable of taking a political position. Thus romanticism seems to be politically neutral and indifferent. According to Schmitt, there are two reasons why this view of the apolitical character of romanticism is mistaken, and both are crucial to the meaning of political romanticism. In the flight from the substance of politics into the fantasies of his imagination, the romantic escapes political reality and remains passive in the face of the forces that define the field of political conflict. He does not develop new ideas or positions. On the contrary, he takes up what strikes his fancy and impulsively discards it when this is no longer the case, only to move on to some other fleetingly more intriguing issue. Thus political romanticism seems to leave everything just as it is. According to Schmitt, this is not the case. In his acceptance of the existing political scheme of things, the romantic implicitly consents to the order that actually obtains. This is why political romanticism amounts to a de facto legitimation of the political status quo and an implicit certification of the political forces that happen to exercise power. Thus from the passivity of the romantic attitude it would be a mistake to infer that political romanticism makes no political difference.

In addition, the possibility of the romantic attitude presupposes a certain kind of political underpinning. When romanticism replaces God — the ultimate principle of traditional philosophical occasionalism — with the individual aesthetic consciousness, this not only secularizes metaphysics but subjectifies and privatizes it as well. According to Schmitt, the elevation of the isolated and emancipated individual to the status of the ultimate metaphysical principle is possible only in the liberal state. The conditions for a perpetual fascination with one's own subjectivity can be satisfied only in the bourgeois social order, which guarantees an absolute dichotomy of public and private spheres. This dichotomy rests on uniform laws that define the private domain and protect it from all interference. These formal, legal conditions for personal security constitute what Schmitt calls the "external conditions" for the preoccupation with private moods that is characteristic of romanticism. Independent of the liberal rule of law and its institution of an autonomous private sphere, the romantic inner sanctum of purely personal experience could not exist. Without the security of the private realm, the romantic imagination would be subject to unpredictable and arbitrary incursions. This means that romantic passivity cannot be apolitical: Romanticism depends upon liberalism.[26] Thus it is no accident that the bourgeoisie of the late eighteenth century became the historical and social bearer of the romantic movement. Only in a bourgeois world can the individual become both absolutely sovereign and thoroughly privatized — not only his own priest but also "his own poet, his own philosopher, his own king, and his own master builder in the cathedral of his personality."

The text

Political Romanticism was originally published in 1919. The ensuing text is a translation of the second edition, 1925, which was revised and expanded primarily through the addition of a new preface and the incorporation of Schmitt's essay "Politische Theorie und Romantik," *Historische Zeitschrift* 123 (1920), 377–97. Schmitt's chapter divisions and subdivisions and his table of contents have been retained. All emphases are Schmitt's. Some of Schmitt's longer paragraphs, which run to two or three pages, have been broken up. In writing *Political Romanticism,* Schmitt was self-indulgent in including many inordinately long footnotes, demonstrating that he had indeed done his homework. These notes cite and discuss a voluminous body of nineteenth-century literature, much of which had become obscure even by 1925. Insofar as these footnotes add nothing of substance to the text, they have been deleted. Notes that are essential either as direct citations or as comments on Schmitt's argument have been retained. Deletion of material from notes is indicated by ellipses. No material has been deleted from the text.

For advice on the translation, thanks are due to D. N. K. Darnoi and Gisela Koch; for advice on the introduction, to G. L. Ulmen and George Schwab; and for research assistance, to Laura Martocci and Gerhard Wagner. This work was supported by a grant from Monmouth College, New Jersey.

Notes

1. Schmitt wrote regularly for the Catholic journal *Hochland* and also for the *Kölnische Volkszeitung*, a daily newspaper with a Catholic orientation published in Cologne. See the following bibliographies of Schmitt's works compiled by Piet Tommissen: "Carl Schmitt-Bibliographie," in *Festschrift für Carl Schmitt zum 70. Geburtstag*, ed. Hans Barion et al. (Berlin: Duncker and Humblot, 1959), 273–330; "Ergänzungsliste zur Carl-Schmitt-Bibliographie vom Jahre 1959," in *Epirrhosis: Festgabe für Carl Schmitt*, ed. Hans Barion et al., 2 vols. (Berlin: Duncker and Humblot, 1968), 739–78; "Zweite Fortsetzungsliste der C.S.-Bibliographie vom Jahre 1959," *Revue européenne des sciences sociales* XVI (1978), 187–238.

2. For recent discussions in English of Schmitt's interpretation of Article 48 and his position on the powers of the office of the Reich president, see Joseph W. Bendersky, *Carl Schmitt: Theorist for the Reich* (Princeton: Princeton University Press, 1983), and Ellen Kennedy's Introduction to Carl Schmitt, *The Crisis of Parliamentary Democracy*, trans. Ellen Kennedy (Cambridge: MIT Press, 1985), xiii–l.

3. *Legalität und Legitimität* (Munich: Duncker and Humblot, 1932), 61. See also p. 37.

4. "Der Missbrauch der Legalität," *Tägliche Rundschau*, July 19, 1932.

5. During Schmitt's rise to academic prominence in the 1920s, his principal mentor and supporter was Moritz Julius Bonn. Schmitt's major treatise on constitutional law was dedicated to Fritz Eisler, a Jewish friend who had died during the First World War. See *Verfassungslehre* (Munich: Duncker and Humblot, 1928). Schmitt also wrote a sympathetic book on Hugo Preuss, one of the chief architects of the Weimar Constitution. See *Hugo Preuss: Sein Staatsbegriff und seine Stellung in der deutschen Staatslehre* (Tübingen: J. C. B. Mohr, 1930). And in 1932, when Schmitt defended the Weimar government in the celebrated supreme court case that resulted when the Social Democratic government of the state of Prussia was removed by presidential decree, one of his partners in the defense was the Leipzig constitutional expert Erwin Jacobi.

6. With the ominous title "The Führer Protects the Law." See "Der Führer schützt das Recht," *Deutsche Juristen-Zeitung* 39 (1934), 945–50.

7. Schmitt seems to have conceived his support for the Nazis as an attempt to protect himself against a despotic and capricious regime that was unable to guarantee his safety. For an account of the motives behind Schmitt's conduct during the Third Reich, see Bendersky, *Carl Schmitt*. The efforts Schmitt was willing to make in order to accommodate himself to the Nazi Jewish policy are nicely illustrated in his book on

Hobbes. This is a purely scholarly work, perhaps the least political of all Schmitt's major books, and certainly not intended for a large or popular readership. Nevertheless, Schmitt cannot forgo a few gratuitously spiteful remarks about Moses Mendelssohn, the Rothschilds, Marx, Heine, and Meyerbeer, and he even resurrects the obscure Jewish thinker Stahl-Jolson as an occasion for flaying the cunning, duplicitous, and opportunistic Jewish mentality. See *Der Leviathan in der Staatslehre des Thomas Hobbes: Sinn und Fehlschlag eines politischen Symbols* (Hamburg: Hanseatische Verlagsanstalt, 1938).

8. *Ex Captivitate Salus: Erfahrungen der Zeit 1945/1947* (Cologne: Greven, 1950), 10–11.

9. *Gesetz und Urteil: Eine Untersuchung zum Problem der Rechtspraxis* (Berlin: Otto Liebmann, 1912).

10. *Der Wert des Staates und die Bedeutung des Einzelnen* (Tübingen: J. C. B. Mohr, 1914).

11. See *Die Diktatur: Von den Anfängen des modernen Souveränitätsgedankens bis zum proletarischen Klassenkampf* (Munich: Duncker and Humblot, 1921) and *Politische Theologie: Vier Kapitel zur Lehre von der Souveränität* (Munich: Duncker and Humblot, 1922).

12. See *Verfassungslehre.*

13. *Die geistesgeschichtliche Lage des heutigen Parlamentarismus* (Munich: Duncker and Humblot, 1923).

14. *The Concept of the Political*, trans. George Schwab (New Brunswick: Rutgers University Press, 1976). The German original is *Der Begriff des Politischen* (Berlin: Duncker and Humblot, 1928).

15. See *Ex Captivitate Salus.*

16. See Søren Kierkegaard, *Diary of a Seducer*, trans. Gerd Gillhoff (New York: Frederick Ungar, 1966).

17. The romantic, therefore, is a paradigm of the coquette, who flirts with reality and transcends its limits by translating all experiences into the domain of the aesthetic. See Georg Simmel, "Flirtation," in *On Women, Sexuality, and Love*, trans. Guy Oakes (New Haven: Yale University Press, 1984), 133–52.

18. For an account of the concept of irony at stake in the literary and political tradition with which Schmitt is primarily concerned, the German romanticism of the early nineteenth century, see Helmut Prang, *Die romantische Ironie* (Darmstadt: Wissenschaftliche Buchgesellschaft Darmstadt, 1972).

19. For the source of Schmitt's concept of the romantic attitude, see Søren Kierkegaard, *The Concept of Irony*, trans. Lee M. Capel (New York: Harper and Row, 1965), "Irony after Fichte," 289–335. This is a revision of Kierkegaard's dissertation for the Master of Arts degree, presented to the Philosophical Faculty of the University of Copenhagen in 1841. Here, all the distinctive properties that Schmitt ascribes to romanticism are clearly set out. Schmitt's treatment of Kierkegaard in *Political Romanticism* is either disingenuous or remarkably obtuse. *The Concept of Irony* and its relationship to Schmitt's own analysis of romanticism are not mentioned. Kierkegaard himself is casually cited in a note as the only great figure among the romantics. Like Schmitt, Kierkegaard was, of course, an extreme antiromantic. He was one of the first acute analysts of the romantic movement and an early explorer of the romantic consciousness and its philosophical, psychological, and sociological bases.

Translator's Introduction

20. Schmitt's view of the exact relationship between decisions and norms was never entirely clear. In the 1920s he attacked the received neo-Kantian practical philosophy and its conception of jurisprudence and politics by arguing that legal decisions cannot be derived from legal norms and political choices cannot be grounded in general moral principles. Instead, norms are instituted or established by decisions. Put another way, norms are decisionistically legitimated: Their binding status as norms is a result of an act of choice between antithetical substantive values. Does this mean that political norms express ultimate commitments that can be explained, mythologized, and legitimated, but not justified? Or can they be pragmatically grounded in the interest in security, peace, order, and stability? Schmitt's writings provide no unequivocal solution to this problem, which is also linked to the issue of the relationship between ethics and politics. Sometimes Schmitt writes as if there is no absolute distinction between ethics and politics, in which case the question of the basis of political decisions in moral principles remains open. On other occasions, he seems to insist on an absolute dichotomy of ethics and politics by banning moral considerations from the sphere of political activity. For an analysis of the shifts in Schmitt's conception of politics that focuses on the problem of the legitimation of political power as the paramount issue in his thought, see Hasso Hoffmann, *Legitimität gegen Legalität: Der Weg der politischen Philosophie Carl Schmitts* (Neuwied and Berlin: Luchterhand, 1964).

21. See Joan Didion, *The White Album* (New York: Simon and Schuster, 1979), 13.

22. For these and other specimens of the age, see Morris Dickstein, *Gates of Eden: American Culture in the Sixties* (New York: Basic Books, 1977).

23. *The Armies of the Night: History as a Novel, the Novel as History* (New York: New American Library, 1968). This book, which was celebrated with great enthusiasm as a path-breaking literary experiment, is an excellent example of the conflation of forms that Schmitt regards as characteristic of romanticism.

24. *The Armies of the Night*, 181.

25. See, for example, Mailer's distrust of the scientific socialism advocated by the orthodox Marxists of the old left, and what he calls "their adoration of the solid-as-brickwork-logic-of-the-next-step." *The Armies of the Night*, 105.

26. This is one of the most important general political implications of Schmitt's argument. Political romanticism is the consummation of liberalism. It is the political ethos that results when the bourgeoisie becomes the bearer of the romantic movement and romanticism becomes the aesthetic of the liberal middle class. Considered in this light, Schmitt's critique of political romanticism is an attack on the modern, romanticized bourgeois order. Schmitt's major political works of the early 1920s are, therefore, linked in the following way. *Politische Theologie* provides a critique of the political philosophy of the preromantic or classical liberalism of the seventeenth and eighteenth centuries. *Political Romanticism* is a critique of the metaphysical and metapolitical bases of modern liberalism. And *Parlamentarismus* is a critique of parliament — the definitive political institution of the bourgeois order — and its viability in the modern liberal state that has been transformed by romanticism. For a systematic discussion of Schmitt's theory of the state and the first attempt in English to provide a comprehensive analysis of his thought and its place in modern intellectual history, see G. L. Ulmen, "The Sociology of the State: Carl Schmitt and Max Weber," *State, Culture, and Society* I (1985), 3–57. This is the first in a three-part series of articles.

Political Romanticism

Preface

Germans lack the facility for making an easily managed, simple name out of a word, so that people can agree without a great deal of difficulty. With us, it is true that an expression quickly becomes banal; but it does not easily become conventional in a practical and reasonable sense. Whatever remains an objective term on the surface, and thus requires a more thorough determination, plods into ambiguities and verbal disputes, and whoever looks for an objective clarification in the confusion soon sees that he is entangled in an endless conversation and a fruitless discourse.

It is not only to us Germans that the theme of romanticism suggests reflections of this sort. The confusion is no less substantial in the French, English, and Italian discussion. And yet here too we feel the verbal facility of the French language and could be tempted to imitate it. Would it not be simple to say that romanticism is everything that can be psychologically or conceptually derived from the belief in the *bonté naturelle* — in other words, the thesis that man is good by nature? This definition — advanced by the French, apparently regarded by them as particularly illuminating, and amplified and documented by Seillière in many books on mysticism and romanticism — actually provides a satisfactory criterion for numerous romantic phenomena and can also be nicely applied to trivial everyday moods and events.

Suppose we imagine someone walking along the streets of a
city or strolling through a market, watching the peasant women
marketing their goods and the housewives doing their shop-
ping, deeply moved by the endeavors of these people in offering one another fine fruits and good food, enchanted by the
charming children and the attentive mothers, the lively youths,
the upstanding men, and the venerable old folks. Such a person
would be a romantic. Rousseau when he paints the state of
nature and Novalis with his description of the Middle Ages
perhaps differ from this person in their literary qualities; but
they do not differ substantively or psychologically. That is because the situation and the theme that are chosen to create a
romantic fable are essentially a matter of indifference. Thus
we meet a succession of well-known figures who qualify as
particularly romantic: the harmlessly childlike primitive man,
the *bon sauvage,* the chivalrous feudal lord, the guileless peasant, the noble robber chieftain, the wandering apprentice and
all the worthy ne'er-do-wells, and the good Russian *muzhik.*
Each of them arose from the belief that somewhere, a natural
goodness of the human being was to be found.

For German sensibilities, such a definition — based on the
thesis of the natural goodness of the human being — has too
much of a moral orientation to the human being. Its historical
orientation is insufficient, and it is not oriented to the universe
at all. It is certainly not the last word about romanticism, and
it is not at all sufficient. That does not mean that we have to
regard this account with disdain. We should at least recognize
that it does not rest content with the superficial general characterizations from which the treatment of the romantic problem suffers. To call romanticism the fanciful, the passionate,
the dreamlike and the poetic, homesickness, the longing for
distant lands, or something of that sort would perhaps itself
be romanticism; but it certainly would not be a concept of
romanticism. It is clearly absurd — although there are examples of this as well — to compile a series of things that are
designated romantic and make a list of "romantic" objects with
a view to possibly deriving the nature of the romantic from
them. The Middle Ages are romantic. This also holds for a
ruin, moonlight, post horns, waterfalls, a mill on a stream, and

many other things that, exhaustively enumerated and combined with the list of romantic figures just mentioned, would produce a very amusing catalog.

It is precisely the futility of such an attempt that should point the way to the correct method. The definition of the romantic cannot proceed from any object or theme that is perceived as romantic, from the Middle Ages or from a ruin. On the contrary, it should proceed from the romantic subject. We will always encounter a certain kind of human being. In intellectual matters, this is obvious. We should attend to the distinctive conduct of the romantic and proceed from the specifically romantic relationship to the world, not from the result of this conduct and all the things and conditions that appear in abundant disorder as a consequence or a symptom.

The thesis of the natural goodness of the human being at least provides one answer. It attempts to understand the romantic manner by reducing it to a formula. The result is at least an approximate determination. This is because every expression in the intellectual sphere has, consciously or unconsciously, a dogma — orthodox or heretical — as its premise. It is precisely the doctrine of the natural goodness of the human being that has proven to be an appropriate criterion for numerous movements, especially when they are linked, as is easily understandable in these cases, with the denial of Original Sin. It is not merely in so-called Rousseauean tendencies — among sentimental anarchists and devotees of humanitarianism — that this sort of dogmatic posture can be recognized as an ultimate motive. It also holds for potent radical movements. The life of many sects — for which Ernst Troeltsch (in his *The Social Teachings of the Christian Churches*) has discovered the formula of the "absolute natural law" — arises from a fanaticism whose anarchical force lies in the denial of Original Sin.

I would regard the explanation based on the thesis of the natural goodness of the human being as both better and more valid than characterizations of romanticism in terms of national qualities, such as the identification of the romantic with the German, the Nordic, or the Germanic. Such definitions of romanticism have been advanced on the basis of quite different motives. On the basis of the viewpoint that the romantic results

from an admixture, romanticism was regarded as the consequence of a fusion of Roman and Germanic peoples; in particular, this sort of admixture was discovered in the so-called
romantic Middle Ages. The Germans then identified the romantic with their own nation in order to glorify both. The
French repudiated romanticism as German and shunted it onto
the enemies of the French nation. On the basis of patriotism,
romanticism can be both exalted and damned. But a great
movement of the nineteenth century that pervades the nations
of Europe cannot be pedantically trivialized by treating the rest
of the world either as a *candidat à la civilisation française* or as
an aspirant to German culture, and by ascribing the predicates
German or *Germanic* to romanticism in addition to those of
fanciful and *passionate*. It is worst of all when such predicates
are intended to serve a pedagogical purpose. On the one hand,
romanticism appears as a new life and true poetry, as the
vigorous and the robust in opposition to the torpor of age. On
the other hand, it appears as a wild outbreak of morbid sensibility and a barbaric incapacity for form. For those who take
the first view, romanticism is youth and health. Those who take
the second view quote Goethe's maxim according to which the
classical is the wholesome and the romantic is the diseased.
There is a romanticism of energy and a romanticism of deca-
dence, romanticism as the immediacy and actuality of life and
romanticism as flight into the past and tradition. Knowledge
of what is essential to the romantic cannot proceed from positive or negative hygienic-moralistic or polemical-political assessments of this sort. It may lead to these assessments as a
practical application. As long as no clear knowledge is established, however, it remains basically arbitrary how the predicates are combined and allotted here and what is singled out
from this extremely complex movement as the truly "romantic"
in order to praise or damn it. Under these circumstances, the
easiest thing to do would still be to follow Stendhal and simply
say that the romantic is what is interesting and the classical is
what is boring, or naturally the other way around. That is
because this tiresome game of praise and blame, enthusiasm
and polemics, revolves around a narrow stick with two ends; it
can be grasped from either side.

In comparison with the foregoing, that definition based on the thesis of the natural goodness of the human being is a commendable and valuable achievement. But it still does not constitute historical knowledge. Its defect is that, as a result of a dogmatic and moralistic abstraction, it fails to recognize the historical distinctiveness of the movement and reduces it, along with numerous other historical processes, to one and the same general thesis. This leads to an unfair rejection of congenial and valuable phenomena and achievements. In this way, harmless romantics are represented in a demonic fashion and placed on the same footing as fanatical sectarians. We have to take every intellectual movement seriously, both metaphysically and morally, not as an instance of an abstract thesis, but as a concrete historical reality in the context of a historical process.

If only a historical description — which is concerned exclusively with the rendition of actual events — remains generally intelligible and internally consistent, no one will demand of it a complete and systematic awareness in the use of language. The situation is different when the aim is to apprehend the focal point of an intellectual movement. For a historical way of thinking that proceeds from such interests, a procedure of taking as the point of departure the opposition of the romantic movement to the Enlightenment and classicism would, in itself, be quite correct. It leads to immense confusion, however, when historians of art, literature, and culture treat this opposition as the exhaustive, definitive criterion. Always with romanticism in mind, they do not derive many historical phenomena from a single general thesis, after the fashion of abstract critics. On the contrary, they relate numerous movements to romanticism, and as a result they discover romanticism everywhere in world history. In this way, religious, mystical, and irrational tendencies of every sort, Plotinus's mysticism, the Franciscan movement, German pietism, the Sturm und Drang movement, all become "romantic."

It is a somewhat peculiar argument by means of which an immense body of historical and aesthetic material is classified in this context in terms of simple antitheses: romanticism or classicism, romanticism or rationalism. Romanticism is the antithesis of classicism. Therefore, everything that is not classical would be romantic — where classicism again signifies a very heterogeneous composite. Sometimes it signifies the paganism of classical antiquity. As a result of this opposition, the Christian Middle Ages would become genuine romanticism and Dante would become the genuine romantic poet. Sometimes classicism is understood as the French art of the seventeenth century, from the perspective of which the German advocates of classicism already qualify as romantics. This is because, in Germany, a classical literature develops out of a polyvalent cosmopolitan movement that was even influenced by Rousseau. And in Russia, where there were no advocates of "classicism" at all, it follows that classicism is something entirely foreign and Western European. Or: Romanticism is the antithesis of rationalism and the Enlightenment, in which case romanticism would be everything that is neither rationalism nor the Enlightenment.

Negative commonalities of this sort lead to unexpected and absurd associations. The Catholic church is not rationalism either, and especially not the rationalism of the eighteenth century. And so it happens that this miraculous structure of Christian order and discipline, dogmatic clarity, and rigorous morality is also declared to be romantic, and the image of Catholicism is also installed in the romantic pantheon along with every conceivable genius, sect, and movement. This is the result of the curious logic that produces definitions by means of an agreement in negation, and in the fog of such negative similarities contrives ever new connections and admixtures. Romanticism made its appearance as a youthful movement in opposition to what at that time prevailed as the old, in opposition to rationalism and the Enlightenment. The Renaissance was also a movement against what seemed in its time to be old and outmoded. The same holds for the Sturm und Drang movement and the Young Germany movement of the 1830s. Such movements appear almost every thirty years. Everywhere in history there is "movement." Thus wherever we look there is romanticism. In the final analysis, however, everything resembles everything else in some way, and the point is not to make an unclear historical complex even more unclear by means of ever new similarities.

I regard this way of proceeding as, for the most part, a consequence of romanticism itself. Romanticism also employed historical events as the occasion for a distinctive literary productivity instead of apprehending them in a matter-of-fact way. Then, however, this productivity itself was also romanticized in such a way that a subromanticism developed. We encounter such a procedure even where we should not expect it. I shall consider only one flagrant example. Giovanni Papini, who understands romanticism correctly as individualism, as a revolt of the ego out of the *spirito di rebellione,* nevertheless begins his description of "romanticism" with the following thesis: There is something vague in this word. But "where we are concerned with phenomena on a grand scale and with colossal movements, nothing is more precise than a vague word."[1] If an opponent of subjectivist tyranny and formlessness and an enemy of romanticism speaks in this way, what can we expect from their friends?

We are all well aware of the imperfection of human language and thought. But even though it would be quite foolish and presumptuous to want to name the unnameable, still it is certain that the core of an intellectual movement must be clear and precisely defined if we are to pass judgment on it and make up our minds about it. To give up on this is really "to trample on humanity." The problem is indeed to achieve clarity, even if it is only clarity concerning why a movement seems to be objectively unclear and why it attempts to make a principle of unclarity. It is inherent in romanticism that it perhaps claims to be incomprehensible and more than human words can intimate. This need not mislead us, for in general the logical tactics of its claim are thoroughly wretched. We need only take note of the way the romantic attempts to define everything in terms of himself and avoids every definition of himself in terms of something else. It is romantic to identify myself with everything, and yet not permit anyone to identify me with the romantic. It is romantic to claim that the Neoplatonic movement is romanticism, occasionalism is romanticism, mystical, pietist, spiritualist, and irrational movements of all kinds are romanticism; but only not the converse — for example, the view that shall be proposed here, that romanticism is a form of occasionalism. For then romanticism itself would be affected in the core of its indefinability. Expressed in a grammatical and logical fashion, this kind of literature always employs romanticism only as the predicate and never as the subject of a definition. This is the simple sleight of hand by means of which romanticism conjures its labyrinth of the history of ideas into existence.

In so doing, romanticism squanders a wealth of discriminating taste and subtle analysis that is often astonishing. All this remains in the domain of a purely aesthetic sensitivity, however, and never forges ahead to a concept. Criticism achieves a more significant depth only when romanticism is historically linked to a great historical structure of the last century. Counterrevolutionary writers in particular have attempted to do this in a way that is often very interesting. In romanticism, they saw the result of the process of dissolution that begins with the Reformation, leads to the French Revolution in the eighteenth century, and is consummated in romanticism and anarchy in the nineteenth century. This is the origin of the "monster with three heads": reformation, revolution, and romanticism. The connection between the first two, reformation and revolution, is well known and extends throughout all the counterrevolutionary thought of the European continent. This holds true not only for France and the genuine political philosophers of the restoration, Bonald and de Maistre, but also for Germany, where F. J. Stahl gave lectures as early as 1853 in order to prove that Luther and Calvin (he already regards the Puritans as doubtful) advanced no doctrine of revolution.

Even during the period of the restoration, romanticism enters this sequence of reformation and revolution. At that time, all good thinkers, liberals as well as counterrevolutionaries, were well aware of the close connection between political-social movements and literary-artistic movements. Donoso Cortés also discusses this in quite axiomatic terms in his essay on classicism and romanticism.[2] He calls literature a reflection of the society as a whole, and he sees that art cannot remain the same when social institutions and sentiments change and are eliminated by a revolution. For him, the question is never a purely literary issue. On the contrary, it is always philosophical, political, and social at the same time. This is because art is the necessary result of the social, political, and religious condition of peoples. For him, romanticism — as was self-evident at that time in France, Italy, and Spain — is a revolutionary movement against traditional forms and existing social conditions. Thus it was condemned as anarchy by the foes of revolution and glorified by its enthusiasts as force and energy. This was the source of the sequence: reformation, revolution, and romanticism. Up to the present day, French royalists have advocated this conception with increasingly rigorous precision, and every day they find new arguments for their thesis. It is a noteworthy symptom that recently this conception has been also gaining ground in Italy, where it has a spirited champion in Papini, and a critic of the importance of Borgese is receptive to it.[3]

The conception is essentially political. It does not explain the striking and characteristic contradictions that the romantic movement exhibits in the political domain itself. On the contrary, it treats the romantic movement summarily as rebellion and anarchy. But how does it happen that in Germany, England, and other countries, people can also have the impression that romanticism is a natural ally of conservative ideas? In Germany, political romanticism is linked with the restoration, with feudalism and estatist ideals opposed to revolution. In English romanticism, political conservatives, Wordsworth and Walter Scott, appear alongside the revolutionaries Byron and Shelley. Cherished romantic objects — the Middle Ages, chivalry, the feudal aristocracy, and old castles — suggest an opposition to the Reformation and revolution. Political romanticism appears as a "flight into the past," a glorification of ancient conditions that belong to the remote past, and a return to tradition. This leads in turn to another generalization: Whoever does not unconditionally regard the present as better, more liberal, and more progressive than earlier times is branded a romantic. This is because the romantic is supposed to be a *laudator temporis acti* or a *prophète du passé*: a eulogist or a seer of times past. In that case, it is precisely those French royalists who would be a model of political romanticism.

Thus a survey of the different possibilities of political romanticism again produces a droll list: the romanticism of the restoration and the romanticism of the revolution; romantic conservatives, romantic ultramontanists, romantic socialists; folk socialists and communists; Marie Antoinette, Queen Luise of Prussia, Danton, and Napoleon as romantic figures. We should add that romanticizing can also work in antithetical directions, treating the same event sometimes in the tones and colors of a transfiguration and sometimes in a dismal mood of horror. One romantic makes the Middle Ages into a paradise. Another — Michelet — makes it into a gloomy vault where there is ghostlike moaning and groaning until the French Revolution shines forth as the dawn of freedom. It is just as romantic to glorify the state because it has a beautiful queen as it is to idolize a revolutionary hero as a "colossus." And yet in political and objective contradictions of this sort, the romantic as such can be quite genuine and invariably the same. This remarkable phenomenon cannot be explained with romantic paraphrases about the contradictions of concrete life. An explanation derived from the concept of romanticism is needed.

This is why a way of thinking that is interested only in politics will never understand political romanticism correctly. Romanticism is not simply a political-revolutionary movement; nor does it lie in a more conservative or reactionary direction. The political conception of the counterrevolutionaries must fall into polemics and arbitrarily ignore considerable parts of the movement; or it must ascribe a malicious and demonic meaning to harmless expressions. In this way, it ultimately suffers from the same defect that is responsible for the inadequacy of the explanation based on the thesis of the natural goodness of man, and it misses the historical core of the romantic. It has nothing to say about the social character of the persons who were the bearers of the movement. For the historical way of thinking, however, this is what really matters.

Every determination of the romantic that offers an answer along these lines is at least worthy of discussion, even if its accuracy and completeness may be doubtful. This is why the view of Josef Nadler deserves special emphasis: because it is based on a genuine definition, and not merely on a characterization or on polemics. Nadler regards romanticism as a folk rebirth, a renaissance. He provides it with a *differentia specifica,* however, and in this way he elevates it above commonplace aesthetic and psychological parallels by characterizing it as the rebirth of a type of people that is historically and sociologically determined, namely, a newly vigorous colonial people. For him, romanticism is the crowning point of the colonization of Eastern Germany, the shifting of formerly Slavic peoples between the Elbe and Memel from East to West, a return to ancient German culture in an area where Germans and Slavs fought with one another. The kind of mentality and renaissance that must develop on colonial soil is in fact different from what obtains where there is a return to a traditional complex of culture, to classical antiquity. The colonial people attempts to make historical and spiritual contact with its own original national past. It was an exceptional service to have perceived and demonstrated the distinctive properties of the colony and the new tribes for literary history. As on every soil, so here as well a unique individuality develops that is transmitted generationally. What Nadler has to say about romanticism is incorporated into his literary history of the German tribes, an important work by a German literary historian. Naturally, the word *romanticism* can be confined to the unique historical and spiritual individuality of the colony and the settlement. But there is a pervasive European romantic movement that Nadler has to ignore if he wants to remain consistent with his definition. K. E. Lusser was correct in pointing this out.[4]

It is not possible to make a comprehensive European movement of the nineteenth century — the totality of which, as was always generally the case, is quite reasonably called romanticism — into something peculiarly German, and then even into an East Elbian phenomenon that would be equated with Brandenburg pietism, Silesian mysticism, and East Prussian speculation. In addition to mystical, religious, and irrational tendencies of all sorts, there were indeed also specifically romantic elements of the large-scale movement whose singularity is to be explained by reference to the Berlin or the East Elbian milieu. They have even become an important impetus for the entire movement; however, no more so than other related phenomena that had nothing at all to do with East Elbia, such as the movement of the French émigrés, who had their most noteworthy representative in Chateaubriand. The colony and the experience of emigration have many things in common. Both can exhibit a special kind of alienation — and even displacement — that can also be observed among numerous romantics. But this is quite peripheral to the movement, and impulses of this sort came not only from Berlin but also, for example, from those French émigrés and from the Irish. The real bearers of the movement cannot be defined by these considerations. A fundamental development quite different from such peripheral events has changed the social conditions of Europe, and a broad stratum has carried on the romantic movement.

✓ The bearer of the romantic movement is the new bourgeoisie. Its epoch begins in the eighteenth century. In 1789, it triumphed with revolutionary violence over the monarchy, the nobility, and the Church. In June of 1848, it already stood on the other side of the barricades when it defended itself against the revolutionary proletariat. As far as I can see, it is most certainly Hippolyte Taine who — relying most closely upon the great sociological and historical work of his own and the immediately preceding generation — has provided a clear historical answer to the romantic problem. For him, romanticism is a bourgeois movement that, in the eighteenth century, prevailed against the dominant aristocratic culture. The signature of the time is the *plebéién occupé à parvenir.* The new romantic art develops along with democracy and the new taste of the new bourgeois public. It experiences the traditional aristocratic forms and classical rhetoric as an artificial model, and in its need for the true and the natural, it often proceeds to the complete destruction of every form. Even then, in 1860, Taine, who articulates this conception in his literary history of English romanticism, saw in the French Revolution the beginning of a new epoch. For him, romanticism signified something revolutionary, and thus an eruption of new life.

His judgment, however, is full of contradictions. Sometimes romanticism is force and energy. Sometimes it is disease and inner strife and the *maladie du siècle.* Kathleen Murray provides a good analysis of the diverse points of view that intersect in his account of English romanticism.[5] Nevertheless, Taine is not refuted by contradictions of this sort, and his work remains exceptionally valuable. That is because he discusses a phenomenon that is intrinsically and radically self-contradictory, namely, liberal bourgeois democracy. When he uses the word *democracy*, he does not at all have in mind the mass democracies of the large, modern, industrialized states. He means the political domination of the liberal middle class, the *classes moyennes*, the class of bourgeois culture and bourgeois property. During the nineteenth century, however, the dissolution of the old society and the development of contemporary mass democracy took place in an unremitting fashion and with great rapidity. As a result, precisely that domination of the liberal bourgeoisie and its culture was eliminated. The liberal bourgeois was never a revolutionary for long. In the nineteenth century, at least in times of crisis, he often stood very insecurely between the traditional monarchy and the socialist proletariat, and in Bonapartism and the bourgeois monarchy he formed peculiar alliances. This is why Taine's judgment must be confused too. For him, the bearer of the new art is sometimes a capable and forceful person whose intelligence, culture, and energy conquer the decadent aristocrats. Sometimes he is an ordinary vulgar moneymaker whose moral and intellectual baseness makes the name *bourgeois* into a term of abuse. Thus Taine wavers between the hope that a new order will emerge from the destruction of the old and the fear that the development will end in chaos, and his judgment on the art of this bourgeois society wavers in the same way. Sometimes romanticism is something great and genuine. Sometimes it is sickness and despair. Today the dissolution of traditional culture and form has continued in a radical fashion, but the new society still has not found its own form. It has not created a new art either, and it continues to move in the discussion about art and in the changing romanticizing of alien forms begun by romanticism and renewed in each succeeding generation.

It is often difficult for Taine to bring off his explanation of romanticism as the art of the revolutionary bourgeoisie. The question of what the politically revolutionary bourgeoisie has to do with the art of Wordsworth or Walter Scott, for example, became all too obvious. In such cases, the French critic avails himself of the claim that here the political movement has "disguised" itself as a revolution in literary style. This explanatory device is entirely characteristic of the sociological and psychological thought of the nineteenth and twentieth centuries. In particular, the economic conception of history employs it in a rather naive fashion when it speaks of the religious or artistic disguise, reflection, or sublimation of economic conditions. Friedrich Engels has provided a paradigmatic case of this phenomenon in his characterization of the Calvinist dogma of predestination as a religious disguise for the relentlessness of the capitalist struggle of competition. But the tendency to see a "disguise" everywhere goes much deeper than this. It does not merely correspond to a proletarian disposition, but is rather of more general significance. To a great extent, all ecclesiastical and state institutions and forms, all legal concepts and arguments, everything that is official, and even democracy itself since the time it assumed a constitutional form are perceived as empty and deceptive disguises, as a veil, a façade, a fake, or a decoration. The words, both refined and crude, in which this is encompassed are more numerous and forceful than most of the corresponding idioms of other times; for example, the references to "simulacra" that the political literature of the seventeenth century employs as its characteristic shibboleth. Today the "backstage" that conceals the real movement of reality is constructed everywhere. This betrays the insecurity of the time and its profound sense of being deceived. An era that produces no great form and no representation based on its own presuppositions must succumb to such states of mind and regard everything that is formal and official as a fraud. This is because no era lives without form, regardless of the extent to which it comports itself in an economic fashion. If it does not succeed in finding its own form, then it grasps for thousands of surrogates in the genuine forms of other times and other peoples, only to immediately repudiate the surrogate as a sham.

Romanticism claimed to be true, genuine, natural, and universal art. No one will deny the distinctive aesthetic appeal of its productivity. And yet considered as a whole, it is the expression of a time that — in art as in other intellectual spheres

— has not brought forth a grand style, a time that, in the pregnant sense, is no longer capable of representation. In spite of all the diversity of judgment concerning romantic art, there is perhaps one point on which we can agree: Romantic art is not representative. And yet this cannot fail to strike us as strange, because romanticism appeared on the scene with great enthusiasm precisely as an artistic movement and a movement in the discussion of art. Romanticism transposed intellectual productivity into the domain of the aesthetic, into art and art criticism; and then, on the basis of the aesthetic, it comprehended all other domains. At first glance, the expansion of the aesthetic leads to a tremendous intensification of artistic self-consciousness. Released from all shackles, art seems to expand immeasurably. An absolutization of art is proclaimed. A universal art is demanded, and everything that is intellectual, religion, the Church, the nation, and the state, flows into the stream that has its source in the new center, the aesthetic. Straightaway, however, a thoroughly typical transformation takes place. Art is absolutized, but at the same time it is rendered problematic. It is taken in an absolute sense, but quite without the obligation to achieve a grand and strict form or manifestation. On the contrary, all of this is rejected, and precisely on account of art, similar to the way that Schiller's epigram professes no religion, and precisely on account of religion. The new art is an art without works, at least without works in a grand style, an art without publicity and without representation. In this way, it becomes possible for art to sympathetically appropriate all forms in a tumultuous disorder, and yet to treat them only as an insignificant model; and ever anew to cry out for the true, the genuine, and the natural in an art criticism and discussion that changes its perspective from day to day.

What at first glance seems to be such a tremendous intensification remains in the sphere of irresponsible private feeling, and the finest achievements of romanticism lie in the intimacy of the emotions. Since romanticism, what does art mean socially? Either it ended in "art for art's sake," in the polarity of snobbery and Bohemianism, or it became a concern of private producers of art for privately interested art consumers. Considered sociologically, the general process of aestheticizing serves only to privatize through the medium of the aesthetic the other domains of intellectual life as well. When the hierarchy of the intellectual sphere disintegrates, then everything can become the center of intellectual life. The nature of everything that is intellectual, including art itself, however, is changed, and even falsified, when the aesthetic is absolutized and elevated to the focal point. Herein lies the first and most simple explanation of the plethora of romantic contradictions that seem to be so complicated. Religious, moral, political, and scientific matters appear in fantastical draperies and in strange colors and hues because, consciously or unconsciously, they are treated by the romantics as a theme for artistic or art-critical productivity. Neither religious, moral, or political decisions nor scientific concepts are possible in the domain of what is exclusively aesthetic. But it is certainly the case that all substantive oppositions and differences, good and evil, friend and enemy, Christ and Antichrist, can become aesthetic contrasts and means of intrigue in a novel, and they can be aesthetically incorporated into the total effect of a work of art. In that case, the contradictions and complexities are profound and mysterious only as long as they are regarded with objective seriousness in the domain to which the romanticized object belongs; whereas we should allow them to have only an aesthetic effect on us.

If these considerations also identify the simple principle in the bewildering disorder of the romantic scenery, the further more important question still remains open: which intellectual structure this expansion of the aesthetic is based on, and why the movement could make its appearance and be so successful precisely in the nineteenth century. As for every genuine explanation, here too the metaphysical formula is the best criterion. Every movement is based, first of all, on a specific characteristic attitude toward the world; and second, on a specific idea, even if it is not always conscious, of an ultimate authority, an absolute center. The romantic attitude is most clearly characterized by means of a singular concept, that of the *occasio*. This concept can be rendered in terms of ideas such as occasion, opportunity, and perhaps also chance. It acquires its real significance, however, by means of an opposition. It negates the concept of *causa*, in other words, the force of a calculable causality, and thus also every binding norm. It is a disintegrative concept. This is because everything that gives consistency and order to life and to what takes place — regardless of whether it is the mechanical calculability of the causal, or a purposive or normative nexus — is incompatible with the idea of the merely occasional. Wherever the opportune and the accidental become principles, an immense preeminence over such binding forces arises. In the metaphysical systems that are characterized as occasionalist because they locate this relation of the occasional at the decisive point — in the philosophy of Malebranche, for example — God is the final, absolute authority, and the entire world and everything in it are nothing more than an occasion for his sole agency. That is a grandiose picture of the world. It magnifies God's preeminence to enormous and fantastic dimensions. This characteristically occasional attitude can persist at the same time that something else — the state, perhaps, or the people, or even the individual subject — takes the place of God as the ultimate authority and the decisive factor. The last of these possibilities is the case in romanticism. Accordingly, I have proposed the following formulation: Romanticism is subjectified occasionalism. In other words, in the romantic, the romantic subject treats the world as an occasion and an opportunity for his romantic productivity.

Today, many varieties of metaphysical attitude exist in a secularized form. To a great extent, it holds true that different and, indeed, mundane factors have taken the place of God: humanity, the nation, the individual, historical development, or even life as life for its own sake, in its complete spiritual emptiness and mere dynamic. This does not mean that the attitude is no longer metaphysical. The thought and feeling of every person always retain a certain metaphysical character. Metaphysics is something that is unavoidable, and — as Otto von Gierke has aptly remarked — we cannot escape it by relinquishing our awareness of it. What human beings regard as the ultimate, absolute authority, however, certainly can change, and God can be replaced by mundane and worldly factors. I call this secularization. That is the issue here, not the equally significant but comparatively superficial cases that directly impress themselves on the historical and sociological observer: for example, the fact that the Church is replaced by the theater, the religious is treated as material for a drama or an opera, and the house of God is treated as a museum; the fact that in modern society the artist, at least in relation to his public, sociologically avails himself of certain functions of the priest, often in a comically deformed manner, and turns a stream of emotions that belong to the priest onto the genius of his own private person; the fact that a poetry arises that lives off cultic and liturgical aftereffects and reminiscences that it squanders away into the profane — and also a music, of which Baudelaire said, in a phrase almost apocalyptic, that it undermines heaven. The transformations in the metaphysical sphere lie even deeper than such forms of secularization, which have been investigated far too infrequently by psychology, aesthetics, and sociology. Here, ever new factors appear as absolute authorities, even though the metaphysical structure and attitude remain.

Romanticism is subjectified occasionalism because an occasional relationship to the world is essential to it. Instead of God, however, the romantic subject occupies the central position and makes the world and everything that occurs in it into a mere occasion. Because the final authority is shifted from God to the genius of the "ego," the entire foreground changes, and that which is genuinely occasionalistic appears in a pristine fashion. It is true that the old philosophers of occasionalism, such as Malebranche, also possessed the disintegrative concept of the *occasio*. However, they recovered law and order in God, the objective absolute. And in the same way, a certain objectivity and cohesion always remain possible whenever another objective authority, like the state, takes the place of God in such an occasionalist attitude. It is different, however, when the isolated and emancipated individual brings his occasional attitude to realization. Only now does the occasional display the total consistency of its repudiation of all consistency. Only now can everything really become the occasion for everything else. Only now does everything that will happen and all sequential order become incalculable in a fantastic manner, which is precisely the immense attraction of this attitude. That is because this attitude makes it possible to take any concrete point as a departure and stray into the infinite and the incomprehensible — either in an emotionally fervent fashion or in a demonically malicious fashion, depending upon the individuality of the particular romantic. Only now does it become clear how much the occasional is the relation of the fantastical, and also — again, varying with the individuality of the particular romantic — the relation of intoxication or the dream, the relation of the adventure, the fairy tale, and the magical game.

A world that is ever new arises from ever new opportunities. But it is always a world that is only occasional, a world without substance and functional cohesion, without a fixed direction, without consistency and definition, without decision, without a final court of appeal, continuing into infinity and led only by the magic hand of chance. In this world, the romantic can make everything into the vehicle of his romantic interest; he can have the illusion, which here as well may be harmless or perfidious, that the world is only an occasion. In every other intellectual sphere, including that of everyday reality, this attitude would immediately become ridiculous and impossible. In the romantic, on the other hand, a special aesthetic achievement takes place: Between the point of concrete reality that serves as an incidental occasion and the creative romantic, an interesting, colorful world arises that often has an amazing aesthetic attraction. We can assent to it aesthetically, but taking it seriously in a moral or objective fashion would call for an ironic mode of treatment. This romantic productivity also treats all traditional art forms as a mere occasion. Thus even though it repeatedly seeks a concrete point of departure, it must alienate itself from every form, just as it does from concrete reality. What has been psychologically characterized as romantic formlessness and the romantic flight into the past or the remote, the romantic glorification of things that are far away, is only the consequence of this attitude. The remote — in other words, that which is spatially or temporally absent — is not easily destroyed or negated, either by the consistency of actual reality or by a norm that ordains compliance in the here and now. It can more easily be taken as an occasion. That is because it is not obtrusively experienced as a thing or an object. This is also because in the romantic, the paramount consideration is that everything ceases to be a thing and an object and becomes a mere starting point. In the romantic, everything becomes the "beginning of an endless novel [*Roman*]." This form of words — which derives from Novalis and recaptures the linguistic sense of the word — is the best characterization of the specifically romantic relationship to the world. It is probably not necessary to add that instead of a novel or a fairy tale, the occasional attitude of the subject can also be manifested by a lyrical poem or a piece of music, a conversation or a diary, a letter, a contribution to art criticism or rhetoric, or, finally, even nothing more than a mood that is romantically experienced.

It is only in an individualistically disintegrated society that the aesthetically productive subject could shift the intellectual center into itself, only in a bourgeois world that isolates the individual in the domain of the intellectual, makes the individual its own point of reference, and imposes upon it the entire burden that otherwise was hierarchically distributed among different functions in a social order. In this society, it is left to the private individual to be his own priest. But not only that. Because of the central significance and consistency of the religious, it is also left to him to be his own poet, his own philosopher, his own king, and his own master builder in the cathedral of his personality. The ultimate roots of romanticism and the romantic phenomenon lie in the private priesthood. If we consider the situation from aspects such as these, then we should not always focus only on the good-natured pastoralists. On the contrary, we must also see the despair that lies behind the romantic movement — regardless of whether this despair becomes lyrically enraptured with God and the world on a sweet, moonlit night, utters a lament as the world-weariness and the sickness of the century, pessimistically lacerates itself, or frenetically plunges into the abyss of instinct and life. We must see the three persons whose deformed visages penetrate the colorful romantic veil: Byron, Baudelaire, and Nietzsche, the three high priests, and at the same time the three sacrificial victims, of this private priesthood.

In the ensuing, the text of the first edition of *Political Ro-manticism*, written in 1917–1918 and published at the beginning of 1919, has been revised and expanded in many — even if not crucial — respects. The essay "Politische Theorie und Romantik" (Political theory and romanticism), published in volume 123 (1920) of the *Historische Zeitschrift*, was incorporated into this new edition. Since the year 1919, the literature on romanticism has increased in an astonishing fashion. In particular, Adam Müller, the German example of political romanticism, has been published in several new editions and celebrated as a pioneering genius. On no account do I see this as a justified response to the objection that I discussed an insignificant and questionable personality such as Adam Müller in far too much detail. The justification is that Adam Müller represents political romanticism as a type with rare purity. In this respect, not even Chateaubriand can be compared with him. This is because Chateaubriand, as an aristocrat and a Catholic from an old family, was always intimately bound up with the things he romanticized. When Müller comes forward as the herald of tradition, the nobility, and the Church, however, the vital incongruity is just as clear as the romanticism. This is the only way that biographical and critical commentaries on Müller's life and works can be justified. The main point was not to unmask a fraud or to "hunt down a poor. rabbit," and even less to destroy a wretched subromantic legend. Indeed, I hope this book remains aloof from every subromantic interest. Its purpose is not to provide the romantic "endless conversation" with a new and perhaps "antithetical" source of stimulation and sustenance. On the contrary, I would like to give an objective answer to a question that is seriously intended.

September 1924

4/2022

Introduction

The German conception: political romanticism as an ideology of reaction and restoration

When Gentz died in 1832, the portents of the year 1848 and the revolution of the German bourgeoisie could already be recognized. The new revolutionary movement understood romanticism as the ideology of its political adversary, reactionary absolutism. Until the work of Rudolf Haym (1870) found a standpoint of historical objectivity, even accounts of romanticism in literary history were filled with political hatred.

After 1815, German liberals linked the restoration, the feudal-clerical reaction, and political subjugation with the spirit of romanticism. Gentz, therefore — Metternich's journalistic aide and a friend of well-known romantics — appeared as the paragon of the political romantic. "Romanticism as a whole, from Schlegel and Gentz to the youngest Young Germans and the most impoverished devotees from the seminaries at Berlin and Halle, or even from the stagnant marshes of Erlangen"[1] — for the young revolutionaries of the period 1815–1848, this was the enemy. This holds true for Gentz especially, the "Sardanapalan" hero of dissolute genius, "the spirit incarnate of Lucinde," the example of romantic insolence whose historical significance lay only in that he combined the political and practical consequences of romanticism in his person and, as a result, sacrificed the labors of a struggle for freedom to the comfortable tranquillity of the reactionary police state.[2] Thus Gentz was dragged in as the romantic through numerous accounts of literary history and politics. Like de Maistre, however, he was gradually recognized as someone completely rooted in the classical character of the eighteenth century. After a reading of his impressive correspondence — publication of which we owe to F. C. Wittichen[3] — no other judgment is possible. His friendship with Adam Müller is an exceptional psychological case. In a sensitive person like Gentz, the acceptance of romantic trivialities proves just as little as it does in the case of Goethe. The decisive matter is the rational clarity of his thought, his reasonable, matter-of-fact attitude, his capacity for legal argument, his sense of the limits of the efficacy of the state, his instinctive animus against people like the Schlegels, and his hatred of Fichte. Intellectually, he belongs to the continuation of the eighteenth century, with Lessing, Lichtenberg, and Wilhelm von Humboldt. Especially in matters of politics and political philosophy, every romantic disintegration of concepts always remained unintelligible to him, and he refused to have anything to do with "fantastic and mystical apothegms and metaphysical fancies," even when they came from his friend Müller. He had a sense for a just "balancing," and during the Metternich restoration — in spite of all his pliancy toward Metternich — he also demonstrated an appreciation for liberal demands as soon as he could only free himself from the fear of a revolution.

At this point, a curious linguistic confusion appears. After the death of Gentz, Metternich wrote to a friend that, in the end, the only services that Gentz performed for him were those of the imagination. He said that Gentz always seemed to him to be free of romanticism, and it was only in the final years that a kind of romanticism could be detected in him. This was, Metternich wrote, the beginning of the end.[4] Here Metternich understands romanticism as the liberal and humanitarian tendencies from which Gentz did not seem to him to be sufficiently free. This was not Metternich's private terminology. On this matter, the aristocrats of the restoration were very sensitive.

Tolerance, human rights, individual freedoms — that was all revolution, Rousseauism, unbridled subjectivism, and thus romanticism.

For revolutionaries of the German reactionary period such as Arnold Ruge, however, this was the essential feature of the romantic, and it often became difficult for them to preserve their terminology, at least superficially, from contradictions. "The basis of all romanticism," Ruge claims, "is the restless, rebellious spirit." This is why romanticism is alleged to stem from Protestantism, the principle of the free self. The connection between Protestantism and romantism is obtrusive. It is not only Catholic counterrevolutionaries who have noticed it, but German Protestants as well. Quite recently, a German scholar observed that the French, "for the best of reasons," felt that there was something Protestant in romanticism,[5] and Georg von Below takes the view that although romanticism "is not a creation of the Protestant spirit, it does qualify as a creation of the soil of Protestantism and its state, Prussia."[6] The antiromantic revolutionaries of the reactionary period only add that romanticism is a ferment of upheaval and caprice, an excessive freedom of the individual who wants to subjugate the world to himself. "Romanticism is the declaration of war by this spirit of caprice — the most offensive, tyrannical, and willful caprice — against the free and lawful spirit of the time." They construed the connection with reactionary politics dialectically, in such a way that although romanticism as negation does indeed include a revolutionary principle, precisely as subjective caprice it is the adversary of the "limits of true freedom," and it repudiates the revolution that issues from the Enlightenment. For the young revolutionaries, the French Revolution was a manifestation of the free spirit. Romanticism was a naturalism without spirituality, substance that does not advance to the concept and self-consciousness. Thus "the endeavors of the political romantics to install the plant or the animal as the ideal for the state and to urge that the state imitate the growth of vegetation and the instinctive movement of the animal organism."

Hegelian constructions of this sort are undoubtedly more profound and correct than the characterizations of romanticism that are commonplace today. And yet they contain an important confusion: Extreme individualism and vegetative torpor are named together as characteristics. In addition, the Hegelians, as representatives of the "real spirit," charged naturalistic romanticism with being a transcendent and abstract withdrawal from real life. Romanticism is alleged to be — as we would probably call it today — a mere wish fulfillment, the illusory satisfaction of a longing that was not really satisfied. As a result, it is explained as a consequence of the wretched political situation of Germany. "Romanticism is rooted in the torment of the earth, which is why one will regard a people as more romantic and elegaic the more unhappy its condition is."[7] The realism of Hegelian revolutionaries was also directed against "Christian" spiritualism and its debasement of reality, and against the lack of "substantiality,"[8] even though they would not have succeeded in capturing their contradictory and multifaceted enemy by means of a succinct concept.

The French conception: romanticism as a revolutionary principle; Rousseauism

For the most part, the insecurity was based on the consideration that the spokesmen for the coming revolution of 1848 idolized Rousseau and the French Revolution and saw here a grand model to which they appealed. In Germany, therefore, they had to contest any connection between romanticism and the spirit of revolution. French writers, on the other hand, have increasingly emphasized this connection, and in the final analysis they have identified revolution with romanticism. The common feature allegedly lies in an individualism that is characteristic of both movements. If we ignore precursors, the opposition to the classicism of the seventeenth and eighteenth centuries begins with Rousseau. Here one saw the renaissance of an individualism and, at the same time, the beginning of romanticism. That is because individualism is "the beginning of romanticism and the chief element of its definition."[9] Because the concept of French classicism — a complex of the seventeenth century — is simple to define historically, it seems that romanticism, as the opposition to the classical, could be more easily defined in France than in Germany, where the classical generation had already grown up under the influence of Rousseau. As a result, the following so-called romantic generation could not base the opposition between the classical and the romantic on such a clear and traditionally established idea of the classic as was the case in France.

Every clear antithesis exercises a dangerous power of attraction over other distinctions that are not as clear. Here the distinction between individualism and solidarity entered the domain in which the opposition between the classical and the romantic obtains. Thus it happens that Ernest Seillière, a French opponent of revolution who dedicated his life's work to the fight against what he called "romantic mysticism," agrees with the German revolutionary Ruge in numerous idioms and arguments. For Seillière, mysticism is an irrational and excessive individualism, the will to power, an expansionist impulse, an imperialism of the single individual as well as of collective individualities, states, races, sects, social classes, or other communities. Romanticism becomes the synonym of mysticism, with a single qualification that is merely historical: Since the eighteenth century, since Rousseau, it is a mysticism that sets itself free from the shackles of ecclesiastical Christianity. The mystical — and, therefore, the romantic as well — appears as a profound impulse of human nature, a general determining factor of human activity, just as elementary as the drive for self-preservation. Man, "by nature evil," is always ready to transgress the narrow limits of what is reasonable — in other words, the limits of the accumulated experience of generations — to create for himself a god as a metaphysical ally, and to subjugate others with the help of this illusion. In aesthetic mysticism, the romantic, who believes himself to be the chosen instrument of a higher power, becomes the artistic genius. As a genius, he finds in himself the only standard of his art. In the mysticism of passion, he declares his lust to be the voice of God. In the mystical religion of the socialist class movement, the proletarian becomes the sole producer of economic values. Finally, a mystical romanticism of race serves the chosen race as the basis for its claim to world domination. Delusion becomes an enormous source of energy and drives the individual as well as entire peoples to extravagant hopes and deeds. All of this signifies "romanticism." For Seillière as well, Rousseau inaugurates modern mysticism, and for him this again means romanticism.

The first romantics had called themselves intellectual revolutionaries. Their historical association with reactionary politics seems to be regarded as one of the many paradoxes that is alleged to belong to the romantic. So, conversely, the association with revolution could also be accidental, and the widespread and simple formula "intellectual or cultural revolution-political reaction" would be a solution. For Seillière, however, it is precisely political revolution that is a manifestation of romantic tendencies, and it is precisely the incalculable political energy of the romantic that disturbs his rationalist empiricism. Here, at least one thing seems to be established: Romanticism combines individualism and irrationalism in itself as its two elements. Unfortunately, that cannot be taken as certain and clear either. The romantics are celebrated by others as the founders of objective historical thought. They are alleged to be the very first to have introduced the appreciation for tradition and to have awakened new sense of community, the first to have discovered "the folk" as an organic, superindividual unity. In Meinecke's famous book on "the genesis of the German national state," they make their appearance as bearers of German national sentiment. Novalis, Friedrich Schlegel, and Adam Müller appear together with Stein and Gneisenau.[10] Georg von Below extols the romantic movement as the true conquest of the rationalist conception of history, as the originator of a new historical sense that has given new life to all historical disciplines.[11] The "endless conversation," a typically romantic idea, and romantic "sociability" are adduced as arguments for the conquest of individualism. Nor can we simply assert that romanticism is the same as irrationalism. Schlegel's *Versuch über den Begriff des Republikanismus* [Essay on the concept of republicanism] (1796) is too deeply grounded in rationalist thought for him to be able to shed it like a piece of dead tissue. On the contrary, often it is precisely intellectualistic and rationalistic elements that have been perceived as essentially romantic.

The explanation of revolution in terms of the *esprit romantique* and the *esprit classique*

Here again, a connection with the French Revolution could be made. Indeed, a historian such as Taine has explained Jacobinism by reference to the abstract rationalism of the *esprit classique*. Narcissistic dogmatists, rendered incapable of any matter-of-fact experience as a result of their *raison raisonnante,* try to form the world according to the axioms of their political geometry. Rousseau moves essentially within the space of this *moule classique,* which becomes increasingly narrow and rigid until eventually a sterile intellectualism destroys everything. Accordingly, what drove on a schoolmaster like Robespierre would not have been the vital abundance of irrational energies, but rather the frenzy of empty abstractness. For Seillière, the revolution is condemned by virtue of the fact that it is irrational. In other words, for him it is mysticism and romanticism. Taine feels himself repelled by its rationalistic abstractness and its *esprit classique.* Thus even though the opposition between classical and romantic seems to be quite simple for French history because a recognized classical tradition exists, the formulas become quite uncertain when they are drawn upon for the explanation of political events. In Taine, moreover, almost all the arguments reappear that were advanced in Germany by opponents of the Revolution who were regularly regarded as romantics. It was not only Burke and his translator Gentz who called the Jacobins mad theoreticians. Adam Müller also characterizes revolution as an idolization of abstract concepts and sets up a connection with the classical era. The latter was the rationalistic absolutism of an individual person. The revolutionary dogma is only the "antithetical chimera" of the same rationalism. In these arguments, Müller is relying simultaneously on Burke, Haller, de Maistre, and Bonald. Therefore, it is precisely the so-called political romantics who see the senselessness of the revolutionary in his remoteness from reasonable experience. It is virtually self-evident that no bourgeois republican in France and no member of the League for the Rights of Man and the Citizen regards himself as refuted by these considerations. Referring to the American constitutions, he claims that although these formulas, which are based "on nature," seem superficially to be abstract theorems, actually they are expressions of sound experience and sound political instinct. It is only in the accusation of romanticism that he pays back his opponents in kind.

The French Revolution is an event that is regarded as a watershed in modern history. Political parties are grouped according to the differing positions they take on the ideas of 1789. Liberals and conservatives are differentiated by the consideration that liberalism has its origins in 1789, conservatism in the reaction against 1789, in Burke and romanticism. The decisive event is characterized in such a contradictory fashion, however, that first the revolutionaries and then the opponents of the Revolution are called romantics. The ideas of 1789 are comprehended in the word *individualism*; and yet the essence of romanticism is also supposed to be individualism. Romanticism is also supposed to constitute a remoteness from reality. But it is precisely the political romantics who, in opposition to the Revolution, appeal to actual experience and reality.

The confusion of the concept of political romanticism and the path to a definition

If, in view of this confusion, we simply gave up any claim to use the word, that would of course be a practical expedient, but not a solution. If the unclear word also moves back and forth in the tactics of political struggles and in the vicissitudes of historical-political discussions, and if it shifts from one side to another in the mechanics of superficial antitheses, still it is necessary — and perhaps also possible — to determine the singularity of what must legitimately be called political romanticism within the historical and intellectual relationships of the complex that is designated as romanticism. The difficulty of providing a convincing definition lies first of all in the fact that *romantic* has not become an accepted name for a political party. As Friedrich Engels correctly notes, "the names of political parties are never entirely right." Words such as *liberal, conservative,* and *radical,* however, have a historically ascertainable and relative content, even though it is not absolute. In such a case, etymology only helps to bring the difficulties to our attention in a forceful manner. Etymologically, *romantic* means *romanhaft*, "fanciful" or "fictitious." The word is derived from *Roman*, a "novel," a "work of fiction," or a "romance." As a differentiation of an epic concept that qualifies as a major term, it could have a pregnant meaning explicable in terms of the word itself. The definition to which the foregoing discussion leads does justice to the meaning of the word and acquires a special justification through the interesting investigations in philological and literary history by Victor Klemperer.[12] Unfortunately, however, the word *romanticism* has been in a state of dreadful confusion for almost a century, an empty vessel filled with contents that change from case to case. In order to elucidate this state of affairs, we may consider the case of an analogous use of another concept that is also epic, that of the "fable." Today, if an artistic or literary movement characterized itself as "fabulous," defined its "fabulous" art as the true, higher, unconditionally genuine and vital, total work of art, and defined the "fabulous" as the higher activity, totality, or metaphysics, if it saw its distinctiveness in being nothing more or less than precisely the "fabulous," then that would certainly call to mind many definitions of romanticism. The movement might possibly succeed and, by means of certain artifacts, give the word a concrete historical content. In that case, it would be foolish to propose that the criterion of fabulous art or the fabulous mode of thought be expunged from the linguistic meaning of the word. It would be even more foolish, however, to see in the program of the movement anything except a rejection of every clear distinction. Therefore, nothing is achieved when the romantic is paraphrased as a mystical-expansive impulse, a longing for what is higher, an admixture of naiveté and reflection, the domination of the unconscious, or in a similar way — not to mention the self-definitions of romanticism ("Romantic poetry is a progressive universal poetry." It "embraces everything that is purely poetic, from the grandest system of art, containing within itself still further systems, to the sigh, the kiss that the poeticizing child breathes forth in artless song").

An additional special difficulty is that it is precisely good historians who — in their antipathy for conceptual distinctions — regard as "romantic" all possible views of a person whom they consider a romantic. For example, because Eichendorff is undoubtedly a good romantic lyricist, it would follow that everything this Catholic nobleman regards as true is also romantic. This is the explanation of an interesting historical phenomenon that Vladimir G. Simkhovitch has pointedly emphasized. "Certain philosophical and literary theories are advanced and advocated by people who hold certain social or political views. Then, by means of a process that can be characterized as substructural," an identification is made. "Thus for decades in Russia, writers who spoke for art for art's sake were immediately perceived as political reactionaries, whereas every realist had to be a liberal or a radical. It was similar in Germany during the first half of the nineteenth century, when romanticism was synonymous with political conservatism, whereas in Feuerbach's decade naturalism was on the same footing as political rebellion and humanitarian socialism."[13]

Thus it is necessary to ascertain what is systematically essential by means of a conscious limitation to a specific historical complex. In opposition to the expansion that the concept of romanticism has met with in the work of Seillière — where it designates nothing more than a general similarity of a psychic habitus in all situations — in the German historians who were concerned with concrete and detailed investigations, one name after the other disappeared from the list that Ruge drew up. Görres was not regarded as a political romantic simply because of his democratic opposition. He could never reasonably be called a romantic, any more than Stahl and Jarcke. And Savigny in particular is excluded as a result of the distinction between historical and romantic political science and jurisprudence. Ultimately, it is only the authentic authors of the political restoration — Adam Müller, Friedrich Schlegel, and Haller — who remain as political romantics.

And yet even this list remains under the influence of the aftereffects of slogans from the period of the German restoration and liberal polemics against "Haller, Müller, and company." The fact that they all became Catholics seemed to provide the basis for a further commonality, which then led to a connection between political romanticism and the "theocratic-theosophic" conception of the state — as if "Roman Catholic" and "theosophic" were not just as antithetical as "classical" and "romantic." But Haller is not a romantic either. His conversion to Roman Catholicism in 1820 has a completely different motivation from that of the twenty-five-year-old littérateur Müller in 1805. If his work made a powerful impression on romantic temperaments of the restoration — on Adam Müller, Friedrich Schlegel, and especially on the Berlin conservative circle — then that could indicate more of an intellectual difference; personalities as unromantic as Bonald or de Maistre also had a decisive influence on the German romantics. Haller has been correctly understood as an intellectual kinsman of Moser. The sober and practical manner in which he holds to the positive reality of a feudal-patriarchal social order establishes that. Insofar as he can be placed beyond these considerations, he belongs to the old deductive tradition of natural law. So among the Germans, it is chiefly Adam Müller who thus far remains as an uncontested example of a political romantic. Along with Friedrich Schlegel and Zacharias Werner, he belongs to the North German Protestant literati who took a southern course and converted to Catholicism. And thus (disregarding Novalis, who died early) he belongs to the party whose path intersected with that of the South German philosophers Hegel, Schelling, and J. J. Wagner, who seem to have taken a northern course, but whose intellectual achievement cannot be defined as romantic. Since Friedrich Schlegel was also politically active and is regarded as a political romantic in the specific sense, he should be considered too.

Before we ascertain the structure of political romanticism on the basis of intellectual-historical and systematic relationships, however, the praxis of a political romantic has to be exhibited by means of an example. For if we are concerned with the crucial singularity of a political expression of life and not with arbitrary constructions, then the way political romantics behave in concrete situations is not a matter of indifference. For Chateaubriand, the reader can be referred to the brilliant account by Paléologue.[14] In Germany, Adam Müller's political activity exhibits the picture that is typical of political romanticism. From this picture, we shall see how mistaken is the currently accepted account that places men such as Burke, de Maistre, and Bonald in the same category of political intellectuality as Adam Müller and Friedrich Schlegel.

4 / 2022

1

The Outward Situation

The personal political significance of romantic writers in Germany

The romantic movement, which made its appearance at the end of the eighteenth century in Germany, declared itself to be a revolution, and thereby established a relationship to the political events in France. In view of the prevailing social conditions in the territories of this movement, in north and central Germany, it was self-evident that the connection was not politically intended. The bourgeois order was so absolutely secure that the enthusiastic reception of the Revolution could be permitted without any hesitation. When the Hanoverian government brought the impropriety of their conduct to the attention of the Göttingen professors Schlözer, Feder, and Spittler — who had used their university chairs to celebrate the liberation of nations from the yoke of tyranny — the professors themselves were obviously surprised to be taken so seriously. If a special satisfaction over the Revolution was manifested at the Prussian Court, that was permitted because, on all accounts, the events in France had to lead to a weakening of the power position of France. Even when the new republic displayed an unexpected military strength and the threatened princes of the Imperial Diet in western Germany proclaimed their fear of the

Jacobin "conquest state" to all the world, still no one expressed any fear of the abstractions of human rights and popular sovereignty that had demonstrated such formidable strength in France. In Germany, it was only in the wake of the wars of liberation that the fear of a revolution by means of ideas circulated and became a pretext for preventive police measures.

When Schlegel claims that the French Revolution, Fichte's *Wissenschaftslehre*, and Goethe's *Wilhelm Meister* were the greatest tendencies of the century or that the French Revolution could be considered the greatest and most noteworthy phenomenon in the history of national states, the political significance of this remark should be assessed in the same way as countless other demonstrations of sympathy by German bourgeois, who allowed events to impinge upon them in the pacified security of the police state and turned the rude realization of abstract ideas that took place in France back into the region of the ideal. It was the reflection of a fire burning in the remote distance. Schlegel also quickly overcame his enthusiasm. It soon happened that the French Revolution was no longer sufficiently grandiose for him, and he noted that an outside possibility for true revolution remained only in Asia. He recognized the French Revolution that actually occurred as nothing more than a gratifying experiment. The revolution of the romantics themselves, however, consisted in promising a new religion, a new gospel, a new creativity, and a new universal art. As regards its manifestations in commonplace reality, scarcely anything belonged in a public forum. The deeds of the romantics were journals. The sensation that certain bourgeois literati created in the salons of Berlin bankers' daughters, the social scandal produced by adultery committed against friends or hosts, the declaration of war against Goethe and Schiller, the destruction of Nicolai and the killing of Kotzebue — these were, taken at their face value, sundry facts. The widely traveled Madame de Staël once expressed her astonishment that in Germany, the most audacious revolutionary ideas were permitted free expression. Of course she also knew the explanation: no one took them seriously. In their politically preeminent position, the nobility and the upper-level bureaucracy did not have to be worried about a few writers who gave lectures under the protection of ladies with literary pretensions — writers who were permitted entree into fashionable society and were passionately bent on assimilating the aristocratic elegance they admired, or at least making a philosophy of urbanity out of it. Baron von Steigentesch, who had the candor of a frivolous man of the world, expressed the typical cavalier's viewpoint: The scholars should only be left to rant and rave at their writing desks. Hunger drives their pens, and here the otherwise dangerous general human impulse for expansion produces only thick books. Even Gentz, who had known how to obtain respect for himself, was at times subjected by Metternich to a friendship that suggests the familiarity between master and valet. It was only to Gentz, his friend and zealous patron, that Adam Müller owed the consideration paid to him. The good Klinkowström was justifiably outraged at the "disgraceful" treatment of Müller and Gentz that the officials of the Vienna Court Chancery permitted themselves. And also in Rehberg's reviews of Müller's lectures we hear the contempt of the sound man. Here the effect is all the more powerful because Rehberg — who did not have the personal antipathy that was displayed by F. Raumer and many others — explains Müller's lecture in a calm, matter-of-fact manner as a consequence of his dependence on high society. But even Lessing might not have been safe from the contempt of uncomprehending aristocrats or bureaucrats. The response to this sort of arrogance and the actual conduct of the political romantic who is given an opportunity for political activity are more important.

Schlegel's political insignificance

In this regard, it is well known that Schlegel had begun by repudiating all practical political work as unworthy, and he had sworn "not to squander faith and love in the political world." When he makes remarks of this sort, however, we should not take Schlegel at his word. Whenever there was something to do, he was keen on entering the fray. His ambition and temperament burned for the business of diplomacy and important commissions. We need not discuss his activity as a war correspondent or his journalistic work as an editor, first of the

Oesterreichische Zeitung, and then of the *Oesterreichischer Beobachter.* Writing certain obligatory articles and memoranda cannot be understood as political activity. After a short time, the real editorial tasks were given to the more able Pilat. The fact that in 1809, Schlegel composed proclamations against Napoleon and even put them up himself does him honor, for it shows that he was capable of a spontaneous feeling. Not until his contribution to the Federal Parliament in Frankfurt, on which Schlegel worked so hard, do we find something that — had it not ended so ingloriously — could be called political activity. Here too, of course, he had begun with grand plans and promises. Dorothea wrote that Friedrich is now "occupied with constitutions and estates, the Federal Parliament, and public affairs," matters only "the future effect" of which would concern their children. He attempted to meddle in diplomatic affairs and tried to outflank his chief, Count Buol, who had entrusted some work to the unemployed Schlegel. On this score, however, he suffered a painful failure. When Metternich in his memorandum of September 16, 1816, requested Buol to endeavor to influence public opinion on his behalf by means of publications and newspapers, he did indeed mention Adam Müller along with Klüber, Nikolaus Vogt, and Saalfeld as writers who might be considered, but not Schlegel. Buol, however, had Schlegel prepare a memorandum. With the exception of this piece and some other works that went unnoticed — the "Bemerkungen über die Frankfurter Angelegenheiten" [Remarks on Frankfurt matters], with which he made a nuisance of himself, some newspaper articles, including one on the Federal Parliament that Gentz described as the work of a "well-meaning dreamer" — Schlegel could not point to any result of his political activity by the time of his recall (April 14, 1818). The correction of the minutes of the Federal Parliament, which he had assumed voluntarily, was soon taken from him. In the end, his letters, like those of his wife to influential acquaintances, are filled with requests for intercession in claims for damages, moving expenses, and the aggressive pursuit of his elevation to the nobility. In addition, there are character sketches of his employers that are of literary interest, and psychological aphorisms and critiques — these, of course, do not alter the fact that his attempt to play a political role failed, just as his appearance in the role of a philosopher in Jena many years before had failed. Finally, Metternich took him along when he left for Rome shortly thereafter, and in his letters he made remarks ridiculing the corpulent and gluttonous Schlegel in a good-natured manner.

From a human perspective and in terms of his intellectual significance, it would be extremely unjust to judge the unfortunate man on the basis of this failure. Nevertheless, where we are to consider the historical impact of the political personality, it has to be noted that whereas most of his political contemporaries had virtually no other immediate impression of his personality beyond that of corpulence, as a politician he was not taken seriously at all. And yet he had made a claim to serious political consideration with his ideas on the papacy, the Church, and the nobility. Here, however, he could not even hold his own against Adam Müller, whom Schlegel as a rule ventured to treat as his intellectual fellow traveler, and concerning whom the overall judgment was given that he was the "shadow" of Friedrich Schlegel.

Müller's political development: an Anglophile in Göttingen, a feudal and estatist-conservative anticentralist in Berlin, a functionary of the absolutist centralized state in the Tyrol

Müller was the Austrian general consul in Leipzig since 1815. Clever and eager to be of service, he had known how to create a sphere of influence for himself there. And yet on one occasion, the forty-five-year-old man wrote to Gentz in a melancholy mood that his rhetorical veins, tapped by newspaper articles, were flowing away and running dry in his "Leipzig salon" for the benefit of a few well-meaning young men, but otherwise without effect. The conclusion of the letter, however, runs differently. Here Müller takes stock of his life. He knows that as a bourgeois without a good name and antecedents, he has managed no small achievement in becoming Imperial general consul in Leipzig. For this he thanks (without a trace of irony) "God and the prince" (Metternich). And yet: "Having arrived seven years ago at the pinnacle of what he could reasonably desire," it pains the bourgeois advocate of the hereditary nobility (whose own elevation to the nobility remained in doubt) that the aristocrats "are so prejudiced against their best defenders," and that the pretensions of birth in Europe "are again becoming quite boastful through our very substantial aid." And on the other hand: "Our prince (Metternich) is happy. Till now, that was my consolation."[1] He had the satisfaction — which was also a political success — that under his influence Duke Ferdinand von Anhalt-Cöthen converted to Catholicism. He lived to experience a recognition that fulfilled his life's wish: his elevation to the nobility. In all this activity, however, he had always remained the unquestioning tool of Metternich, and when he "strayed," this did not happen in political praxis, but rather in theoretical intimations made in his writings. At the end of his life, he was simply a good, pious Catholic, frequently so meek that he probably paid for a human judgment with a decade of doubtful ambiguity. But the period in which he could make autonomous political decisions lies in the years 1808–1811. At that time it was still possible for him, as it was for Gentz, to become the spokesman for an important political idea, and to seek out and inspire a public on its behalf. In this way, he could have legitimized himself as a political journalist, and he also could have legitimized his own distinctive contribution as a political idea. If we view these years without concentrating unduly on biographical matters, then their outcome is the following.

Adam Müller also began as a romantic rebel, even though he already played the foe of the French Revolution as a twenty-year-old student in Göttingen. He did this as a docile follower of Gentz and by way of assuming a pose of Anglophilia, which he adopted under the influence of the Göttingen milieu, whose "cultural physiognomy at that time was more English than German."[2] Continental romanticism always had a strong propensity for Anglomania. But it is important for an understanding of the romantic character that the influence of English culture that at that time emerged so powerfully in Hanover had nothing to do with romanticism. This influence was based on the solidarity of the reigning dynasty, common social interests, and the thorough familiarity with the English character and English institutions possessed by intelligent high officials such as Brandes and Rehberg. The kinship of Lower Saxon and Anglo-Saxon stock strengthened this influence and eliminated the last remaining vestige of the suspicion that romantic impulses could be at stake here. Thus the Hanoverian University of Göttingen also maintained its distance from the enthusiasm for the French Revolution, and many scholars adopted a prudent and critical posture in relation to the important events of the time. In the flood tide of Kantian and post-Kantian transcendental philosophy, "common sense" remained academically respectable at Göttingen.

The impression produced by these reasonable and objectively grounded influences of the English character was romanticized as Anglomania in the young Berliner. The son of an insignificant head of a finance office attempted to play the rich Englishman to strangers, and even at the beginning of his career he exhibited the inclination to quickly adapt himself to the ideal of social elegance that prevailed in his surroundings. At the same time, for him England was the homeland of philosophy. It was even the place where the arches of the academy he meant to establish would rise up. In addition, his interests retained the kaleidoscopic quality of romanticism: economics, philosophy of nature, medicine, literature, and astrology. His first book, *Die Lehre vom Gegensatz* [The theory of polarity] (1804), exhibits this quality of many-sidedness intact. It is a quality that could leave no object of interest untouched; nor could it apprehend any in an objective fashion, and it culminated in the attempt to meld Burke and Goethe into a higher third factor. Burke was the exponent of the English romantic complex, Goethe the exponent of the German. Müller treated neither as a real person, but both as romantic figures, and thus they could easily be melded. This is because the author was a romantic. In the preface, he began with the premise that the Revolution had failed. At that time, in 1803, this was the view of Schlegel as well. "Philosophical systems," he claims, "shattered crowns, republican constitutions, theo-philanthropic plans, wrecked enterprises for preservation as well as destruction, moral principles and textbooks on natural right, exhausted duties, and abandoned rights lie together in one vast rubbish heap; and to this date no text, no discourse, no deed that the tumultuous conclusion of the eighteenth century left behind for us is complete." Under these circumstances, the young writer wanted to reinstate the wrecked enterprise of the Revolution and carry it to its conclusion, give the words *religion, philosophy, nature,* and *art* a new content, break through the boundaries of the previous mechanistic age, and transplant the ethereal speculations of the intellectual revolution into the soil of reality.

In the ensuing years, his ideas did not become clearer. And his social and economic circumstances were such that his ambition must have been frustrated by this fact. He lived with his Polish friends Kurnatowski and Haza, who had also made him the "delegate" of their South Prussian Economic Society. One need only look at the "annals" of this association of rural landed proprietors in order to see that it could not satisfy a young man consumed by the desire to play a role in the real social world. In the melancholy of a lonely residence in the country, he suffered from severe depressions. He felt ill, became disagreeable, pursued astrology and meteorology, and finally accepted the invitation of Gentz to go to Vienna (from February 8 to April 30, 1805). There he converted to Catholicism on the day before his return journey. In October of 1805, he moved to Dresden with the Hazas, with whom he also lived, and as an unaffiliated scholar he gave lectures together with Böttiger and G. H. Schubert to a fashionable audience composed mainly of foreigners: in the winter of 1805–1806, on German literature, science, and language; in 1806–1807, on dramatic poetry and art; in 1807–1808, on the idea of beauty. The lectures also appeared in book form and in part they were printed in *Phoebus,* the journal that Müller had edited together with Kleist since January 1808. The success of these lectures was quickly forgotten. Müller contributed several essays to *Pallas: Eine Zeitschrift für Staats- und Kriegs-Kunst* (edited since 1808 by Rühle von Lilienstern), including some remarks "Bei Gelegenheit der Untersuchungen über den Geburtsadel von Fr. Buchholz" (On the occasion of the investigations concerning the hereditary nobility by Friedrich Buchholz), in which he defended the nobility against the attacks of Buchholz.

At this point, his faithful friend Gentz, who was always concerned about Müller, gave him a decisive push and suggested that he write a book in defense of the nobility, or perhaps publish a collection of political, moral, and historical essays. "With heart and soul, I assure you that you will make an enormous reputation for yourself — and should you decide for the first course (the defense of the nobility), you will establish an extremely agreeable existence for yourself."[3] Gentz's plan was based on the calculation that a faction that had fallen into difficulties with public opinion — such as the German, and especially the Prussian, nobility — would be grateful for any journalistic support. As a result of the defeat of 1806, liberal reforms that conflicted with the interests of the hereditary and landed nobility were to be expected in Prussia. Müller, of course, counted on entering the service of the Prussian nobility. Nevertheless, he agreed to his friend's proposal and attempted to achieve both aims with one stroke. As early as the winter of 1808–1809, he gave lectures in Dresden on "das Ganze der Staatskunst" (Statecraft as a whole), in which he interceded on behalf of the feudal nobility and at the same time offered a series of political and historical remarks. The lectures were held "before His Serene Highness Prince Bernhard von Sachsen-Weimar (Müller had been appointed his tutor) and an assembly of statesmen and diplomats." He published them under the title *Elemente der Staatskunst* [Elements of statecraft], in which there might be an allusion to Euclid's *Elements of Geometry*. Here, too, Müller's success was limited to a narrow circle of acquaintances.

Meanwhile, Müller had gone to Berlin in the spring of 1809 because his presence in Dresden had become impossible. In the first place, for social and moral reasons: He had run away with the wife of his friend and host of many years, and shortly thereafter he married her in Berlin; but then for political reasons as well. It was not as if, like Kleist or the young Dahlmann, patriotism had made him give way to incautious remarks or actions. In his lectures on statecraft, all clear references to the time, and on several occasions even the word *French*, were deleted. They were subsequently reintroduced into the Berlin printing. So perhaps this was a measure imposed by the censor.

In *Elemente der Staatskunst,* he makes malicious remarks at the expense of the people of the Alliance for Virtue. He speaks of their "theatrical melancholy," in which they "certainly fancy themselves as refined," and, probably in an allusion to Kleist, speaks of the "ideas of murder and revenge with which they are flirting." He treated the worthy Martens — who delivered a letter from Count von Götzen and wanted to inform himself concerning the state of the national movement in Saxony — with an arrogant civility that was ridiculous and offensive at the same time. When the French marched into Dresden, however, he had to flee, because shortly before this, while the Austrians were in the city, he had made himself too visible publicly on behalf of their interests. And yet this catastrophe was not the kind that would have permanently compromised him in "higher places" either.

In Berlin, he submitted an interesting suggestion to the Prussian government (in a letter of August 20, 1809, to his acquaintance the privy counselor for finance, Stägemann). With excellent observations on the advantages of a semiofficial newspaper, he expounded the necessity for a regular influence of the government on public opinion. At the same time, he had an ingenious plan for sabotaging the opposition by forestalling them. He wrote verbatim: "I venture to publish a government newspaper openly and with the authority of the Privy Council, and to publish a popular newspaper anonymously and with the mere connivance of the Privy Council: in other words, to write both a ministerial and an opposition newspaper."[4] In this letter — and also in the "Memoir concerning the Publication of a Prussian Government Newspaper," which he submitted a few weeks later — he repeatedly emphasized his main concern: that he would be able to perform all these important services only if the government secured a social position for him in order to put him in touch with the most important and the most favorably disposed men of the kingdom. The Prussian government accepted the plan of establishing a government newspaper. For Müller, the enterprise began in a promising way. In some newspapers, notices already appeared in which he was named as the editor of a Prussian government newspaper that would appear shortly. When Hardenberg became chancellor, however, Müller was no longer under consideration for the editorship of the paper. It is true that Müller had promised to defend Hardenberg's policies as a journalist, and for this he was assured of receiving an annual retainer of 1,200 taler from Hardenberg. Over and above this, however, he demanded a secure position as a higher official of the Prussian government. Hardenberg, who knew something about the untrustworthy and superficial littérateur, refused. At that same time, Müller had also made connections with the agrarian-conservative opposition. As early as the beginning of 1810 (from January 11 to March 29), he gave lectures on Frederick II in which, with clear allusions to "clever thinkers," he spoke against all liberal reforms. Meanwhile, the estatist opposition developed further and gained important social and intellectual support in the Christian German Dinner Club, in whose foundation Müller had taken part. Müller's *Elemente der Staatskunst* became a kind of programmatic text for this circle. Here and in the *Abendblätter* that Kleist edited beginning in 1810, Müller took on a spirited role in the struggle against the "fashionable" reforms and the "Anglomaniacs" and Smithians. He made spiteful allusions to the chancellor and his colleagues, and through his essays on the Finance Edict of October 27, he aroused anger and exasperation in government circles.

Müller also drafted the memorandum of February 11, 1811, that was submitted by von der Marwitz, the leader of the estatist opposition. He even wrote on the fair copy, so that Hardenberg, who knew Müller's handwriting well, was aware of Müller's role in the affair. The flattering remarks about Hardenberg — which, in spite of all this, were scattered throughout the memorandum — did not fail to produce an advantageous impression for Müller. Quite guilelessly and without any sense of his political opportunism and lack of character, Müller continued to maintain his relations with Hardenberg, continued to collect his retainer, and by means of a sudden article eulogizing the chancellor, let it be understood that he would be quite prepared to represent a different standpoint in exchange for a suitable post in the Prussian government. The chancellor did not feel moved to enter such a game of "polarities." Nevertheless, by means of some well-considered and friendly gestures, he pursued the matter somewhat further through Gentz. Because of his economic predicament, Müller was forced to pursue an opportunistic policy. When he realized that he would accomplish nothing with the chancellor, he hastened to Vienna, to his old friend and supporter Gentz. This is where he remained after his final attempts to get a position in Prussia had proven to be futile.

Here we should stress that Müller did not turn from Protestant and liberal Prussia to traditional, Catholic Austria because of an antirevolutionary instinct. On the contrary, until the last moment, he tried to find a position in Prussia, and indeed with Hardenberg. The only condition that he insisted upon was a respected social position. He went to Vienna only because Gentz could be of further use to him there. In Berlin, he maintained a prudent silence about his conversion to Catholicism and concealed it in general idioms that, at the time, were modern. The charter members of the Dinner Club, people like Arnim, could allow themselves an open expression of their sympathy for Catholic ways. The son of the finance officer Müller, however, who wanted to obtain a post as a higher official at any price, would have utterly compromised himself in Berlin with an avowal of Catholicism. That is why he placed this side of his life in the background.

For the rest, his political debut began with a pose that was not altogether honorable. In 1808 when he appeared in the lists against Buchholz in order to defend the nobility, he stressed with a fine emphasis that the nobility had no need to defend itself against attacks such as those of Buchholz. He was only concerned that the middle class was defamed by such vulgar attacks. He ventured into a controversy with Buchholz only to defend himself and the affront to his middle-class status, whereas for him (Adam Müller) as a rule, it was only opponents such as Montesquieu and Burke who made a controversy worthwhile. The dishonesty is not in the way Montesquieu and Burke are alluded to here. This was romantic presumption, which was only particularly careless in political discussion. But consider the contempt with which nobles and bourgeois must have treated a man who for years had lived off the tables of certain aristocrats and then dared to come forth as the champion of the honor of the middle class. Perhaps this also explains why he impressed so many of his contemporaries as a liar. We will find very few examples of someone who so universally seemed false to his fellow men. And indeed, this does not turn on the gossip of letters and diaries in which romantic garrulousness is mirrored, but rather on serious utterances. Rehberg's view has already been cited. Solger speaks of a "fraudulent adulteration." Wilhelm Grimm claims that everything worthy in Müller is "borrowed," and in a letter to his brother, he writes openly: "Do you not also feel that a certain lie is propagated through all his writings?" And Alexander von der Marwitz agrees with Rahel that Müller is a "dishonorable and mendacious fellow," "lazy and irreligious," and concerned only with his "distinguished role."[5]

The picture would be incomplete if we did not also consider for comparison Müller's activity in the ensuring years, 1813 to 1815. At that time, he had the opportunity of proving in practice his position as the representative of Burke in Germany and his views on the necessity of estatist and corporate privileges, the utter inadequacy of the mechanistic-centralistic administration of the state, and all finance measures reckoned solely on the basis of fiscal revenues — views put into play in his opposition to Hardenberg in Berlin. During the war of 1813, Roschmann, the provisional head of the province, had taken him along to the Tyrol as aide-de-camp and journalistic attaché. After the conquest, the province was to be reorganized. The central government in Vienna expected from the province not only the highest revenues possible but also its "Austrianization": in other words, its incorporation into the centralized system of the state as a whole and the elimination of the estates and their privileges: estatist rights to tax concessions, an autonomous military security system, and an independent influence on legislation concerning police and the administration of justice. Roschmann, an ambitious careerist — in the diary of the Archduke Johann, he is simply called the Sneak — wanted to use this opportunity to become governor of the Tyrol. Thus he carried out the intentions of his superiors ruthlessly, and wherever possible he even exceeded their wishes. In particular, it was important to appear in Vienna as an acute financial expert who did not support the military force intended for the Tyrol through the general funds stipulated for that purpose, but rather covered the expense from the province itself. The important movement of the Tyrolean people that aimed to restore the ancient special privileges was suppressed, and in the reports to Vienna it was systematically distorted. As regards the Tyroleans, the method of this policy consisted in the ruthless collection of the "oppressive and unpaternal" taxes imposed by the Bavarian government, a consumption tariff on Bavarian grain, disciplinary measures against the inhabitants for "seditious" complaints, and a system of police spies.

Müller supported his chief, Roschmann, by means of proclamations, memoranda, and newspaper articles (in the *Boten von Südtirol*). On the whole, he has to be seen as the one with the intellectual initiative, for Roschmann was entirely dependent on his help. In the reports that went to Vienna, the "useful services" of Müller are prominently lauded. Müller was happy that the emperor, Metternich, and Baldacci — the last being a particularly energetic advocate of rigid bureaucratic centralization — were satisfied with him. "As far away as Naples and Geneva, it is not easy for an interesting person to escape me, and I shall never regret my acquaintance with this remarkable country," he wrote to Gentz. "The most interesting tasks fall to me by the natural force of gravity. I would hope that the compensation would take the same direction." As he expressed it, his objective was "not to cauterize the proud flesh of the Tyrol and Italy, but rather to restore it to the main body."[6] When Roschmann finally had to leave the country, he petitioned Archduke Johann expressly, asking that Adam Müller be recalled too. On April 23, 1815, Müller was called to the Imperial headquarters, just as his 162-page memorandum — which mentions the suspicious tendencies of the Tyrolean people and suggests that estatist aspirations be eliminated by means of strict measures against the nobility and the peasants — was on the way. Thus ended Müller's activity among this people, who believed — on the basis of dynastic loyalty proved in 1809 — that they had a claim to a consideration for traditional special privileges, and whose geographic, economic, and historical peculiarities would certainly have to be respected by a herald of "local characteristics."

The false accounts Müller later gave about his importance in Berlin and the conceited representations he made about his accomplishments in the Tyrol should not deceive us. All in all, he was nothing more than a zealous servant of whatever system happened to be in power, always ready to discard that part of his ideas which might stand in the way of its smooth functioning and to assimilate the rest. He made some reservations only in the Catholicism of his later years. Under the circumstances of the restoration, however, this required no exceptional resolve. In the enthusiasm of his zealous officiousness in the Tyrol, he had at first written: "I should really have been in the Commission for the Reform of the Cloisters. If the old Holy Man really had a mastery of the world, if he knew what his Jesuits should reply when a fractious scholar interrogated them closely about their ossified and stale philosophy, then no power on earth would have been able to exclude Consalvi from the restricted Congress." Here, however, the Catholic church turned out to be the rock on which romantic vanity — which proposed to enlighten everybody concerning their true character — was shattered. After the Napoleonic Wars, the powerful religious movement — which again led many, both Catholics and Protestants, to a pious and informed Christianity — took place in Germany. It stirred not only romantics and apocalyptics, not only the followers of Madame Krüdener, but also the unstable Fessler in his faraway Sarepta, and the worthy Kanne in Erlangen. It made them into devout Protestants. This movement touched Müller, who had already taken the path to Catholicism, and it carried him inwardly to the ultimate consequences of his path, to an orthodox religiosity for which even Görres was no longer sufficiently absolute, and which rebuked Haller's book on the restoration because it did not proceed from the premise of divine revelation. Here Müller gradually ceases to behave as a romantic. In any case, it is a mistake to call him a romantic on the grounds that he was a Catholic. This popular conception is to be explained only as a consequence of that dilettante's conflation of romanticism with the romanticized object. Catholicism is not something that is romantic. Regardless of how often the Catholic church was the object of romantic interest, and regardless of how often it also knew how to make use of romantic tendencies, the Church itself was never the subject and bearer of a romanticism, no more than this was the case for any other world power.

5/2022

2

The Structure of the Romantic Spirit

La recherche de la Réalité

The philosophical problem of the age: the opposition of thought and being and the irrationality of the real

Here we have to ignore all the petty treacheries and human frailties that one finds in the life of the political romantic. The rootlessness of the romantic, his incapacity to hold fast to an important political idea on the basis of a free decision, his lack of inner resistance to the most powerful and immediate impression that happens to prevail at the time — all these things have their individual reasons. If they are to be relevant for a definition of political romanticism, then they must not be psychologically or sociologically derived, but rather placed in the context of the intellectual situation. Then it will become evident what a foreign element is and what is essential to the romantic movement. The romantics took an interest in all conceivable historical, political, philosophical, and theological themes, and they participated ardently in the philosophical discussions of their time. This is why Fichte's philosophy of science and Schelling's philosophy of nature are frequently classified as romanticism. The reciprocal personal and intellectual influences are well known and have often been investigated. The result was ever new connections, new dependencies, new sources, and new confusions. Romanticism became the philosophy of nature, mythology, and irrationalism, without placing the distinctiveness of its intellectual situation in relief in a pregnant fashion. The elucidation of romanticism, like that of every important situation of modern intellectual history, must begin with Descartes.

At the beginning of modern intellectual history, there are two major transformations that together form an interesting countermovement. In the Copernican planetary system — to whose revolutionary significance Kant was fond of referring — the earth had ceased to be the center of the universe. With the philosophy of Descartes, the convulsions of ancient ontological thought began. The Cartesian *cogito ergo sum* argument referred the person to a subjective and internal process, to his thought instead of the reality of the external world. Natural science ceased to be geocentric and sought its focal point beyond the earth. Philosophy became egocentric and sought its focal point in itself. Modern philosophy is governed by a schism between thought and being, concept and reality, mind and nature, subject and object, that was not eliminated even by Kant's transcendental solution. Kant's solution did not restore the reality of the external world to the thinking mind. That is because for Kant, the objectivity of thought lies in the consideration that thought moves in objectively valid forms. The essence of empirical reality, the thing in itself, is not a possible object of comprehension at all. Post-Kantian philosophy, however, made a deliberate attempt to get a grip on this essence of the world in order to put an end to the inexplicability and irrationality of real being. Fichte eliminated the schism by means of an absolute ego. As absolutely active, it emanates in the world and posits itself and its antithesis, the nonego. In contradistinction to this sort of systematic simplicity, Schelling's answer was uncertain. But it followed the path to external reality that was sought. It was the return to nature, only in a philosophical sense, of course. Fichte's "annihilation of nature" was opposed to Schelling's position. Fichte could not place the absolute in nature either, however, for he also started from transcendental critical philosophy. Thus he designated the absolute neither as subjective nor as objective, but rather as the point of indifference between the two. Absolute reason had two poles: nature and mind. Philosophical reality is neither the thinking intellect nor the external world, but rather an indifferent, absolute, third entity. To call it reason already manifests a dubious inclination to subjectivity.

Four different modes of reaction against modern rationalism

Romanticism can be conceived as a movement that opposed the rationalism of the eighteenth century. But there were many such countermovements. They were quite diverse, and it would be superficial to call romantic everything that does not qualify as modern rationalism. In Schelling's philosophy of nature, there was a philosophical opposition that romanticism perceived as "wisdom without love." The common opposition to abstract rationalism notwithstanding, emotional opponents were distinguished from philosophical opponents. That is evident, for a purely emotional treatment of philosophical problems is not possible, and every systematic treatment is, once more, an intellectual performance. This is because every attempt at philosophical systematization threatens the unqualified immediacy of feeling. Experience, which is infinitely self-sufficient, again appears threatened in an intellectualistic fashion. Fichte's philosophy of science already includes a philosophical reaction to Kantianism. The ego that, absolutely active, "posits" the nonego is not a concept in the sense of the analytical concept of a rational logic, the concept that ascends to abstract generalities. It is a concrete, individual concept that emanates in a concrete world.

In the fundamentals of his philosophy of science, Fichte had admitted that the systematic part of his doctrine would be Spinozism, except that each and every ego would itself constitute the highest substance. As a result, the duality of abstract concept and concrete being characteristic of abstract rationalism was surmounted and the "vital unity" won. In Fichte's work, however, the old rationalism is still paramount. The ego, which enters a causal relationship with the nonego, sees in the latter a "modifiable material," something to be manipulated and transformed in a rational fashion. Then of course Schelling construed the idea of the "organism" as a totality that supersedes the schism of nature and mind. The great systematic consummation is not achieved, however, until the philosophy of Hegel: The absolute subject, in a process of becoming, emanates itself in antitheses. Now Schelling feels an affinity for Spinoza, with whom the entire German "philosophy of emotion," and especially Jacobi, is in sympathy. Herein lies an important correspondence. Namely, the systems of post-Kantian idealism comprise a philosophy of intuition and a pantheistic rationalism. It is with an emanationist concept (here borrowing an expression from Lask: a concept that concretely posits concrete individuality) that they react against an abstract rationalism that admits only analytical-abstract concepts — concepts that, for this reason, never arrive at concrete individuality. Spinoza's system, however, is the first philosophical reaction — and one analogous to this post-Kantian reaction — to the modern abstract rationalism defended at that time by Descartes and Hobbes, to a mechanistic world view. The characteristic schism that clearly emerges not only in Descartes but also in a particularly interesting form in Hobbes — between a phenomenalism that regards the external world as pure perception and an equally unqualified materialism that admits only corporeal movements — is surmounted. Thought and being become attributes of the same infinite substance.

In addition to this philosophical struggle for the reality that is inaccessible to abstract rationalism — a struggle that reached its peak in Spinoza and Hegel — three other oppositions are discernible. In their premises, methods, and results, they are utterly different, and yet they are all directed against the rationalism inaugurated by Descartes. First, there is antiphilosophical mysticism. It has its inspiration in two women, Madame Guyon and Antoinette Bourignon, and its apologists in two earlier philosophers, Fénelon and Poiret (the advocate of a "religious realism"). In the nineteenth century, a movement that was also very powerful, although its results were certainly less original, would correspond to this tendency. Its most conspicuous figure is also a woman, Madame Krüdener;

in addition, however, a manifestation as typical as the sudden turn toward pietism taken by Kanne, the most important advocate of a philosophy of nature, should not be overlooked. As regards the political consequences of these two forms of reaction, emanationist philosophy can probably be allied with conservative results. Following the examples that Hegel, Schelling, and J. J. Wagner provided at the beginning of the nineteenth century for the application of the idea of the "organism" to the existing conditions of the old German empire, emanationist philosophy even seems to be particularly suited to conservative results. This is because the "state," the concrete state that exists historically, is no longer to be juxtaposed in an abstract fashion to the idea of the state, represented as the preeminent reality from which the individual only emanates. On the other hand, the mysticism just discussed — to the extent that it is not absolutely quietistic, indifferent, and "apathetic" — exhibits a clear propensity for social criticism. Its apocalyptic elements can support a powerful revolutionary chiliasm, and if it treats the human understanding in a nihilistic fashion, then that easily turns into a political and social nihilism. In Bourignon, many revolutionary remarks can be pointed out, of which the most interesting is this: Cartesian science was invented by the rich in order to deceive the poor (in other words, it is something like a "class ideology"). Here, not only a political revolution but also a social revolution is proclaimed. In this mysticism, the opposition to the abstract and mechanistic rationalism of Descartes is just as powerful as its opposition to the pantheistic rationalism of the "atheist" Spinoza.

In addition to these two countermovements, which are obviously different from each other — namely, (1) the philosophical and (2) the mystical-religious countermovements — there are two other independent forms of reaction that differ from each other just as clearly: namely, (3) a historical-traditionalistic reaction that is represented by Vico and directed against the antitraditional tendency of Cartesian rationalism, and, finally, (4) an emotional-aestheticist (lyrical) reaction, whose first independent expression is found in Shaftesbury. This last reaction does not set up a philosophical system. It rather transforms the oppositions it sees into an aesthetically balanced harmony.

In other words, although it does not produce a unity from the dualism, it reduces the oppositions to aesthetic or emotional contrasts in order to fuse them. It is not in the position of providing an independent refutation of rationalism. It turns the pregnant concepts of the philosophy of the time back into the domain of the emotional, for example, making the innate idea into an innate feeling. Nor does it mystically abandon or transcend the world. That is because — remaining in the world, but always with a longing for the Other and the Higher — it always finds the way to urbanity. The origin of romantic irony lies in this suspension of every decision, and especially in the vestige of rationalism that it reserves for itself in spite of its thoroughly irrational bearing, the origin of this clear criterion that immediately makes the difference from mysticism evident, since there is no ironic mysticism. The decisive opposition lies in the consideration that mysticism, as Christian Janentzky aptly formulates it, is a "manifestation of the *religious* consciousness,"[1] whereas this fourth form of reaction essentially belongs to the sphere of the aesthetic. It develops the distinctively romantic feeling for life and nature. When it undertakes to articulate itself intellectually (and in spite of an apparent intellectuality, which is actually a cerebral sensualism, it simply cannot do this on the basis of its own distinctive presuppositions), this feeling mingles heterogeneous concepts from philosophical systems — nature, *logos*, the ego — with sentimentalized concepts of the time. This feeling, however, has its own distinctive mode of productivity, namely, the lyric. Lyrically and sentimentally, it perceives the systematic rationalism of the political philosophy of Hobbes as particularly hostile. In the first place, the anti-idyllic idea of a person who is "evil by nature," a struggle of all against all, and free competition are repellent to this feeling. Thus Shaftesbury already celebrates the simple, "natural" customs of primitive peoples, and he especially stresses their musical gifts. It is not until Rousseau, however, that the singularity of this fourth form of reaction emerges more clearly. Incapable of surmounting rationalism and always intellectually dependent upon the superior opponent (*The Social Contract* proves that), he still manages to paralyze the consistency of rationalism and to arrive at con-

crete reality — which philosophy seeks by pursuing a system-
atic-speculative path — in another way. Thus far, the
prototypical singularity of the path on which he arrives at this
result has hardly been noticed. But it can already be discerned
in the *Discourse on the Origin and Foundations of Inequality*. "Nature," a thoroughly rational idea of traditional philosophy, a
synonym for the conceptual, rational "essence," for reason and
nomological regularity, acquires a sentimental content. The
"state of nature" of earlier philosophy, which was treated as an
intentional abstraction or a historical fact, becomes a concrete
idyll that takes place in forest and field, a "romantic fantasy."

The German romanticism of the beginning of the nineteenth
century belongs to this fourth form of reaction. In it, ideas of
Hemsterhuis, Herder, Hamann, Jacobi, and Goethe are placed
in the service of the aesthetic reaction, even if, as S. Elkuss has
correctly noted, in a "literarily diluted" fashion.[2] It should also
be noted that the concepts from the philosophy of the time
that German romanticism made the object of its emotional
reversal were in part drawn from Kantian philosophy, but in
part from the philosophical systems of Fichte and Schelling as
well — in other words, from systems that were already expressions of reaction. As a result, the intermixing that necessarily
takes place in the aesthetic-emotional rejection of every logical
distinction becomes even more opaque, and the confusion
seems to be inextricable.

In historical reality, the four forms outlined here are seldom
present in prototypical clarity. Vico, for example, reproaches
Descartes not only for an ahistorical and untraditional abstractness but also for the prosaic quality of his work. In Fénelon,
there are pronounced elements of Neoplatonism, mediated by
the influence of Malebranche and Augustine. Shaftesbury's
connection with Malebranche has not yet received anything
like enough attention. Spinoza's philosophy contains enough
mystical elements to be in accord with the second form of
reaction; and the publications of P. M. Masson make it sur-
prisingly clear how profoundly Rousseau is connected with the
quietism of Guyon, a point that is admirably stressed by Seillière. In the German romantics, the intermixing is even more
pronounced. Novalis — assuming that we propose to under-

stand a young man in terms of such categories — is sometimes a mystic and sometimes a romantic; he came from the circle of the Moravian Brethren, whose religiosity was regarded with suspicion by the Lower Rhine mystics as "sweet experiences." In the cases of Friedrich Schlegel, Zacharias Werner, and Adam Müller, apocalyptic moods are evident, after such moods, independent of them, had appeared throughout Europe. In the relations of Brentano with Katharina Emmerich, we find analogies to the friendship between Poiret and Antoinette Bourignon. The so-called political romanticism of the restoration is dependent upon the historical reaction to abstract rationalism, upon Herder — who, on the basis of interests in cultural history and not romantic interests, arrived at a different estimation of the Middle Ages — and upon Bonald. Burke would have to be mentioned here too. This liberal contains romantic elements himself, however, and he marks a historical connection between the Whig aristocrat Shaftesbury and the German romantic Adam Müller.[3] In spite of these considerations, the types remain easy to distinguish. They are set out here in order to show the extent to which the rejection of rationalism is motivated and formed by varied factors, and how a first distinctive feature of the romantic already results from these considerations. For the further determination of romanticism in intellectual history, however, a more important point should be noted, a change that occurred because the metaphysical development from the seventeenth to the nineteenth century led to entirely new ideas of God and the absolute.

God, the highest reality of the old metaphysics, and his representation by two new realities: humanity (the people) and history

The highest and most certain reality of traditional metaphysics, the transcendent God, was eliminated. More important than the controversy of the philosophers was the question of who assumed his functions as the highest and most certain reality, and thus as the ultimate point of legitimation in historical reality. Two new worldly realities appeared and carried through a new ontology without waiting for the conclusion of the epistemological discussion: humanity and history. Completely irrational when considered in terms of the logic of the rationalistic philosophy of the eighteenth century, but objective and evident in their superindividual validity, in reality they dominated thought as the two new demiurges. The first, human society, came to the fore in different forms: as the people, community, and humanity, but always with the same revolutionary function.

Humanity as the revolutionary demiurge, history as the conservative demiurge

Its omnipotence was already proclaimed in Rousseau's *The Social Contract*. It can lay claim to everything because the social contract contains in itself "the total alienation of each associate, and all his rights, to the whole community, every individual giving himself up entirely." In practice, the individualistic elements that lay in the contract theory were thrown aside in the Revolution. Politics becomes a religious matter. The political organ becomes a priest of the republic, the law, and the country. It was with bloody zeal that Jacobinism raged against all political dissidents and every divergent opinion. Its fanaticism had a religious character. The new cult of freedom, virtue, or the "supreme being" was its natural consequence. Even Aulard admits that.[4] Every political enemy — Danton and Hébert — was a rebel against the sole and supreme sovereign, and thus an "atheist." In this case, it may be that a frightful human egoism and a mad will to power made use of an ideology in order to rage unchecked. That has often been the case in human history. The decisive factor is this: Here, it appealed successfully to a new religion. When an absolute monarch says that he himself is the state and when a Jacobin acts as if he could say *la patrie c'est moi*, this is not the same thing. The one represents the state with his individual person. The other substitutes his person for the state. The more he himself wants to be, all the more must he conceal his private person and always emphasize vociferously that he is only the functionary of the sole, powerful, authoritative, and superpersonal being. Even if he were different from the strict moralist Robespierre and were driven by exclusively egoistic motives, he could permit himself to enjoy private advantages, power, honor, and wealth only casually, as an insignificant byproduct, and in an underhanded and thievish fashion. For himself, he is nothing. He is everything in his function as the agent of true power, the people, or society. With the desire to return to nature, society was discovered. The reality was the human community, from which the sentimental individualist believed he was fleeing.

From the standpoint of his Christian political philosophy, Bonald saw the Jacobinism of 1793 precisely as the eruption of an atheistic philosophy. He had worked out an analogy between the theological and philosophical idea of God and the idea of the political order of society. It led to the conclusion that the monarchist principle corresponds to the theistic idea of a personal God because it requires a personal monarch as a visible providence. A monarchist-democratic constitution is supposed to conform to the deist assumption of a transcendent God. An example is the Constitution of 1791, according to which the king was just as powerless in the state as the God of deism was in the world. For Bonald, that is crypto-antiroyalism, just as deism is crypto-atheism. The "demagogic anarchy" of 1793, however, was open atheism: no God and no king.[5] This "identity in the principles of the two societies, religious and political," has its justification in the methodological identity of numerous theological and legal concepts, especially constitutional concepts. It should not be confused — no more than the parallels between philosophy and jurisprudence that Leibniz set up — with the frivolities of theosophy and the philosophy of nature, which find colorful analogies for the state and society just as they do for everything else. This identity was intended as a justification for monarchism and the aristocracy. It included, however, the recognition of a new reality in the form of the nation. As of 1796, the reproach that Bonald raises against Descartes and Malebranche runs as follows: They do not see what is essential, human society. Society and history, that is reality.[6]

In de Maistre, the recognition of this reality is equally positive. Like Burke and Bonald, he repeatedly emphasizes that the individual person can create nothing, but can only "fabri-

cate" something, whereas law, constitutions, and language are
products of human society.[7] The nation is, of course, a creation
of God. But if his argument is examined more closely, this is
the decisive point. In a letter to Count Blacas, he summarized
the quintessence of his argument in the following terms: "No
public morality or national character without religion. No European (!) religion with Christianity. No Christianity without
Catholicism. No Catholicism without the pope." Even during
the Revolution and the rule of Napoleon, his strong national
feeling never wavered. It was self-evident to him that France
had to defend the integrity of her borders, even if by means
of revolutionaries; and in the matter of the Sardinian policy,
he was a good Italian. Here, however, the only issue of interest
is what he sees as the cardinal point of his argument and, at
the same time, its incontestable premise: public morality and
national character are what everything depends upon. Christianity becomes a European religion. The papacy legitimizes
itself by virtue of its indispensability for national character.
Catholicism is a national element of France and is rejected as
the state religion only because experience shows that if it is
limited to a state, the practical effect of religion cannot take
place. The nation must renounce Gallic Catholicism, but in its
own interest.

For these opponents of revolution, human society already
contains a historical determination. It has become the nation.
Without this, the unlimited community is essentially a revolutionary god that eliminates all social and political barriers and
proclaims the general brotherhood of humanity as a whole. If
the removal of all limits and the need for totality were sufficient
in itself to define the romantic, then there would be no finer
example of a romantic politics than the resolution of the National Convention, which on November 19, 1792, decrees "that
it will grant fraternity and aid to all peoples who want their
liberty, and it charges the executive power to provide the gen-
erals with the orders necessary to aid these peoples." Such a
politique sansculotte abolishes all national boundaries and inun-
dates the *politique blanche*, the international policy of the Holy
Alliance and the legitimist status quo.

The corrective to revolutionary license lay with the other, second demiurge, history. It is the conservative god who restores what the other has revolutionized. It constitutes the general human community as the historically concretized people, which becomes a sociological and historical reality by means of this delimitation and acquires the capacity to produce a particular law and a particular language as the expression of its individual national spirit. Therefore, what a people is "organically" and what the *Volksgeist* signifies can be ascertained only historically. In addition, here the people is not its own master, as in Rousseau, but rather the result of historical development. The idea of an arbitrary power over history is the real revolutionary idea. It has as its content "fabricating" whatever it wants, and being able to create itself. It can, of course, be found in any human activity. The unrestrained fanaticism of the Jacobin was "unhistorical" thought. The quietism of the restoration period could justify itself with the claim that everything that happens is good because it is a historical event. What exists is rational because it is the work of the world spirit that produces itself historically. What history has done is done well. The *voluntas Dei in ipso facto* (the will of God in the very fact itself), which earlier could justify everything, had to give way to historical justification *ex ipso facto* (from the very fact itself).

We should not, however, understand every historical point in an isolated fashion and in terms of itself. Otherwise we would be back in the atomistic-analytical rationalism of the eighteenth century. Only in duration does time approach the irrational abyss that brings forth the cosmic event out of itself. The appeal to duration is the received conservative and traditionalist argument. It is only the condition of continuous duration that justifies every state of affairs. Time immemorial as such is the ultimate basis of right. For the state, the importance of both religion and aristocratic families is that they give it a duration, and only thereby does the state acquire its reality.[8] When the conservative Bodin opposes Machiavellian power politics on the grounds that it considers only immediate utility and in the long run would lead to misfortune for the state, this is still a sober and practical objection that gives a mere experience its due without systematically making duration the basis of justification. The extent to which Gentz still stands in the eighteenth century becomes clearly evident only when he discusses duration. He simply wants to say that in the assessment of political events, we have to bide our time. It is the sensible wisdom: *tempus docebit* [time will teach us]. Now, however, time as history becomes a creative power. It carries peoples and families to world-historical greatness. It forms nations and individuals. In it, humanity grows. De Maistre found grandiose words for the grandeur of the process in which a new family makes its appearance in world history and comes to power. He even uses the phrase *legitimate usurpation* (in other words, a usurpation that is historically durable), which is intelligible only on the basis of the new historical sensibility and threatens his entire doctrine of legitimacy as a system and a principle. And Bonald said that reality is in history. Burke also had repeatedly alluded to the character of the nation as an enduring community that extends over generations. He sees the justification for entailments in the fact that the duration of the state rests on them; the justification of Church properties in the fact that they make possible farsighted plans that have to take long periods of time into account. In Burke, however, all this remains on the level of practical reflections. The idea of the new power that, as such, can justify something is not present in his work, although there is hardly a single material argument in the entire historical school of law that would not already have turned up in Burke. In light of this consideration, however, the pathos with which he stands for the great, superindividual national reality, independent of all the power and volition of the individual person, is all the more effective. The idea of ascribing a special character, a *Volksgeist*, to peoples was nothing new. That had already been done in Voltaire, Montesquieu, Vico, and Boussuet, and Malebranche, Descartes, and Bodin were all familiar with it.[9] The new element was this: Now the people becomes the objective reality; historical development, however, which produces the *Volksgeist*, becomes the superhuman creator.

In Schelling ("in history, it is not the individual who acts, but rather the species"), the superindividual reality was still essentially defined by considerations based on the philosophy of nature. It was not historically oriented. Hegel was the first to bring the two realities into one synthesis, and thereby to consistently take the step that inevitably dethroned the God of traditional metaphysics. The people — which in Hegel had been rationalized into the state — and history, the world spirit that develops itself dialectically, are united, in such a way, of course, that in Hegel's metaphysics, the *Volksgeist* functions only as an instrument of the logical operation of the *Weltgeist,* or world spirit. Empirically and psychologically, however, the latitude that remained to the *Volksgeist* was broad enough so that politically, Hegelianism could have a revolutionary tendency in addition to its reactionary tendency. Even in the articulation of Hegel's system, human society remained the revolutionary ferment. In the revolutionary development of this system, in Marxism, the people in the form of the proletariat again appeared as the bearer of the true revolutionary movement, which identifies itself with humanity and understands itself as the master of history. Otherwise Marxism would be a philosophy of history like others, without revolutionary force and the power to form a party following. But there was no longer any way back to the traditional God of Christian metaphysics, in spite of the reactionary elements and the Christological terminology of Hegel. Stahl demonstrated his preeminence when he confidently recognized Hegelianism as the enemy of that which is old and is based on a Christian foundation. His starting point was the philosophy of Schelling, which in 1809 had returned to the acknowledgment of a personal God.

The romantic subject and the new realities

Stahl was not a romantic. The essential feature of the intellectual situation of the romantic is that in the struggle of the deities he does not commit himself and his subjective personality. His position is the following. Under the impression of Fichte's individualism, the romantics felt strong enough to play the role of the creator of the world themselves, and to bring forth reality out of themselves. At the same time, they were the heralds of the two new realities, community and history, to whose power they immediately succumbed. In the trenchant phrase of S. Elkuss, however, all this served them only as "an intellectual means of strengthening the sovereignty of the ego." Instinctively, they left unclear the extent to which the romantic ego identified itself with the new powers or made use of them as instruments of its own power. When the genial subject seriously put its divine autarky into practice, it no longer tolerated any community. The incorporation of the subject into community and history meant that the self as creator of the world was dethroned. In the Catholic church, the romantics found what they were looking for: a vast, irrational community, a world-historical tradition, and the personal God of traditional metaphysics. Everything together — this is why they were able to believe that they were becoming Catholics without having to make a decision. For the romantics, herein lay the mystery and the magnetic force of Catholicism. But when they were also inwardly overwhelmed by Catholicism and seriously wanted to be pious Catholics, they had to give up their subjectivism. This they did, after they had tried for some time to play the genial subject in relation to the Church as well (just as Adam Müller wanted to interrogate the Jesuits and their "stale philosophy" with his theory of polarity). With the definitive renunciation and the perception of an either-or, the romantic situation was brought to an end.[10]

The opposition of possibility and reality

Nevertheless, in order to understand the romantic situation and the romantic significance of the two new realities, a complication must be considered that arises out of the romantic conflict between possibility and reality. Romanticism began as a movement of the young against the old. It is natural for the rising generation to look for a grand slogan for its opposition to the old generation in power. It cannot always take this slogan from finished achievements, which is why this generation makes an appeal to its youth as such, to the active, to its own energy and vitality: in other words, to its possibilities. The rising generation is always storm and stress. It introduces new ideals and thereby creates a place for its accomplishments, as a result of which the following generation again regards it as belonging to what is old. The romantic generation, the end of the eighteenth century, was in an especially difficult situation. They were confronted with a generation whose achievements were classical; and in response to its greatest representative, Goethe, the only productivity they had exhibited was an admiring and intense enthusiasm. Their output lay in the domain of criticism and character sketches. All their pretensions that lay beyond that were mere possibility. They made audacious plans and bold promises. They made intimations and held out prospects. They responded to every expectation of a fulfillment of their promises with new promises. They withdrew from art into philosophy, history, politics, and theology. But the enormous possibilities that they had opposed to reality never became reality. The romantic solution to this difficulty consists in representing possibility as the higher category. In commonplace reality, the romantics could not play the role of the ego who creates the world. They preferred the state of eternal becoming and possibilities that are never consummated to the confines of concrete reality. This is because only one of the numerous possibilities is ever realized. In the moment of realization, all of the other infinite possibilities are precluded. A world is destroyed for a narrow-minded reality. The "fullness of the idea" is sacrificed to a wretched specificity. In consequence, every spoken word is already a falsehood. It limits unbounded thought. Every definition is a lifeless, mechanical thing. It defines indefinite life. Every foundation is false; for with the foundation, a limit is always given as well.

Now, therefore, the relationship is reversed. It is not possibility that is empty, but rather reality, not abstract form, but rather positive content. This also signifies a reversal philosophically. The age sought reality in order to put an end to the mysterious irrationality of real being. Should that occur by means of a process of rationalization, then the infinity of life would again be eliminated, for in this way it would again be conceptually defined and limited. The meaning of all the ingenuity of the philosophers, as well as the overheated cerebralism of many romantic utterances, is that they wanted to grasp existence and explain it without forgoing the thrill of untouched possibilities. No argument on this point, however, can address the problem posed by the fact that the person who argues employs a rational, and not an irrational, faculty. Intellectual intuition, a genial flight of fancy, or any other intuitive process might also be mentioned by means of which special insights not accessible to the mere understanding (in Schlegel's terminology: to mere reason) were to be obtained. But as long as there were pretensions to a philosophical system, the contradiction within the system could not be overcome. As long as, in the manner of romanticism, fragments and aphorisms were to mediate the results of intuitive activity, however, this amounted to nothing more than an appeal to the same activity on the part of like-minded souls; in other words, an appeal to the romantic community. The goal of all philosophical endeavor — to reach the irrational philosophically — was not attained. In a special form, the new reality, society, had prevailed over the romantics and had forced them to appeal to it.

Romanticizing the people and history

The opposition of the possible and the real is fused with the opposition of the infinite and the finite, the intuitive and the discursive. Here, too, the mystic of the Middle Ages, who traced the problem back to the conflict between the modalities, again found the resolution of the conflict in God. Only God is infinite possibility and, at the same time, each concrete reality. He unites in himself *posse* and *esse,* what could be and what is, as the suspension of all the oppositions of the infinite and the finite, motion and rest, possibility and reality. As the curious form of words employed by Nicholas of Cusa has it, he is the *Possest*: the unified identity of possibility and actuality. That is a mystical resolution, but it is not romanticism. Here, too, the romantic attitude is that of the subject that does not commit itself. What the medieval mystic had found in God, the romantic subject attempted to take upon itself, but without giving up the possibility of assigning to the two new demiurges, humanity and history, the problem of such a unification.

In Rousseau, the people is already powerfully sentimentalized as an emotional community, and the romantic, who began as an individualistic rebel, appears as a collectivist. The vast, superhuman collective individual in which thought and life are one, the good, noble, magnanimous people, confident in its instincts, becomes the reservoir of all the irrationality of the infinite unconscious and, at the same time, the reservoir of the spirit. The people as it really exists was assigned the task of becoming the bearer of the naiveté that the romantic had lost in his own person. It became the faithful, patient, even-tempered, unassuming people, for which the impatient, nervous, and pretentious intellectual was touched with admiration. Figures out of Rousseau — the honest artisan, the generous laborer, the wise old man, the virtuous housewife — appear in all romanticism, and even the journalist of the Metternich restoration, Adam Müller, wrote in 1819: "The simple farmer daily influenced by the seasons and the blessing of God, the peaceful artisan, the insignificant member of the community — they are the upholders of our ranks and our freedoms, they preserve the sentiment that made Europe great." Not even the nobility is mentioned here. For political reasons, he avoids the word *people*. Nevertheless, the romantic function of the people is just as clear here as it was ten years earlier in his *Elemente der Staatskunst,* where he invariably refers to the state instead of the people and exalts the state as the ultimate ground of all possibilities. Its will is law and the voice of truth, not merely legally but in fact. Müller built a romantic theory of paper money on Novalis's idea that the greater the demands are that the state imposes on the individual, the more it is cherished. The new reality of the "people," however, should not be confused with the "people" as a romantic object, and the romantics should not be regarded as the discoverers of the new popular or national feeling. That is because they quickly attempted to romanticize the reality. The essential difference is already contained in the significant avoidance of the word *people* in that remark by Müller: The revolutionary nerve is cut out of the romantic object. This object is at the disposal of the romantic subject, which assigns it the task of being the source of unexhausted possibilities. In practice, it has the obligation of keeping its distance from the Enlightenment, because reading and writing and the entire fraud of education would destroy the vast domain of the unconscious.

Children are also bearers of the irrational profusion that the romantic has at his disposal. Not every child; as Novalis said, not "spoiled, pampered, namby-pamby children," but only "un-determined children." Like many other romantic sentiments, this one as well had already been expressed by Schiller in his essay on naive and sentimental poetry: What is touching about a child is that it is not yet determined, not yet limited. It still has in itself all the innumerable possibilities that the man has already lost. Primitive peoples — humanity as childlike — are also bearers of these unlimited possibilities. The contradiction between rational limitation and the irrational profusion of pos-sibilities is romantically eliminated because another equally real but still unlimited reality is played off against limited reality: in opposition to the rationalistic, mechanized state, the childlike people; in opposition to the man already limited by his profes-sion and accomplishments, the child who plays with all possi-bilities; in opposition to the clear line of the classical, the primitive in its infinity of meanings. Limited reality is empty, a realized possibility, a decision that has already been made; disenchanted, disillusioned, it has the dull melancholy that a lottery ticket has after the drawing. It is "a calendar whose year has expired." Primitive naiveté is the happiest state, but only negatively and not because of a positive content. It is the illusion not yet destroyed, the eternal promise of eternal power, an eternally conserved, because eternally unrealized, possibility.

The second of the two new demiurges, history, can be turned to a romantic use as well. In every moment, time determines the human being and confines the most powerful human will. As a result, every moment becomes an overwhelming, irra-tional, ghostlike event. It is the ever-present and incessant negation of the countless possibilities that it destroys. In the face of its power, the romantic yields to history. The past is the negation of the present. If the present was negated possibility, then in the past the negation is negated once again, and the limitation is nullified. The bygone fact has the existential qual-ity of the real. It is concrete and actual, not capricious poetry. And yet it does not have the obtrusiveness of present reality, which in every moment oppresses the romantic as the individual person who exists. To that extent, it is both reality and irreality. It can also be interpreted, combined, and construed. It is congealed time with which one can undertake to make marvelous figures.

Reality that is spatially remote can also be used as a way to escape the reality of the present. In his Berlin lecture of 1802, A. W. Schlegel stated that, to the French, at least before the war, England had been the romantic land where noble lords came from. In the same way, when both the English and the German novelist strive for the extraordinary, they like to shift the scene to southern Europe, to Italy or Spain. In the mechanics of this romantic change of place, the most banal novelist does not differ from the pretentious romantic littérateur. Time, however, is better suited to the irrational factor of romantic opposition than space, for the latter immediately suggests a rationalization. Thus at the turn of the eighteenth century, the romantic escapes into the Middle Ages. This is because at that time, during the French Revolution and the Empire, the flight into classical antiquity remained too close to the present, which clothed itself in the garb of ancient Rome. As a romantic alibi, Greece could do better. In any case, the following always remains essential to the concept of the romantic: The temporally or spatially remote romantic object — regardless of whether it is the glory of classical antiquity, the noble chivalry of the Middle Ages, or the powerful grandeur of Asia — is not of interest for its own sake. It is a trump card that is played against the commonplace, actual reality of the present, and it is intended to negate the present. The remote, the unusual, the fantastical, the protean, the marvelous, the mysterious that some people even incorporate into a definition of the romantic, have no intrinsic importance. Their romantic function is the negation of the here and now.

Regardless of how conversant the romantic is with the idea of the person who is good by nature, and with the idea of the primitive people, the sons of light, the genuine priesthood, earliest humanity, and the lofty, natural wisdom of antiquity, and regardless of how often this is linked with their romantic critique of the present, the religious or mystical idea of the lost paradise still differs from the romantic idea. Religious and

mystical ideas, gnostic ideas as well as traditionalistic arguments, can be drawn into the service of the romantic attitude.
The past appears as the better foundation of the present.
Indeed, the present becomes a parasite of the past. "We still
live off the fruit of better times" (Novalis). "We are consuming
the capital of our fathers" (Müller). What is romantic in this is
only the use of the past as a negation of the present, as a way
out of the prison of the reality that is concrete and present.
This is not experienced in a Buddhist fashion. The romantic
does not escape into nothingness. On the contrary, he seeks a
concrete reality, but it is a reality that does not disturb and
negate him. And in spite of the claims of the liberal Hegelians,
this has no intrinsic relations to Christian transcendence either.
That is because the other world of Christianity is a world in
the hereafter. Its terrible decision — eternal bliss or eternal
damnation — turns all the fits of romanticism into an absurd
trifle. Although its heaven is indeed filled with music, the Last
Judgment stands before this eternal harmony. Moreover, this
is not the romantic world of another time and another place.
Finally, the romantic world is not utopian either. That is
because utopia lacks the most important factor: reality. It
is supposed to become real. But this is not something that
interests the romantic. He has a reality that he can play out
today. He does not want to be bothered with the task of a
concrete realization.

Irony and intrigue

When Goethe withdrew from the commotion of political events
into the "patriarchal atmosphere" of the Orient, that could be
called an escape. Morally we can qualify this however we like,
but it is not romantic. It has been set down as a distinguishing
mark of the romantic that he is always in flight. That touches
the essential point just as little as explanations in terms of the
longing for higher things, or other accounts of the same sort.
The romantic withdraws from reality. He does this ironically,
however, and in a spirit of intrigue. Irony and intrigue do not
constitute the state of mind of a person in flight, but rather
the activity of a person who, instead of creating new realities,

plays one reality off against another in order to paralyze the reality that is actually present and limited. He ironically avoids the constraints of objectivity and guards himself against becoming committed to anything. The reservation of all infinite possibilities lies in irony. In this way, he preserves his own inner, genial freedom, which consists in not giving up any possibility. By this means, however, he also defends himself against the objection that would necessarily destroy his pretensions: that all the promises and the grandiose projects he has opposed to the limited achievements of others are unmasked as a fraud by his own real production. For him, the concrete accomplishments that are actually at hand amount to nothing more than byproducts. He protests against having himself or any of his proclamations understood within the limits of current reality. This is not what he is. This is not his ego. At the same time, he is still infinitely many other things and infinitely more than he could ever be in any concrete moment or specific expression. He regards being taken seriously as a violation because he does not want the actual present confused with his infinite freedom.

Arnold Ruge, an enemy of the romantics, held the view that Platonic — that is, Socratic — irony did not leave off being bonhomie. Schlegel's irony, on the other hand, was a "cliquish persiflage." That holds true only in particulars. From the standpoint of its genesis, romantic irony is a residue of rationalism. That is because romanticism cannot decide between rationalism and irrationalism, no more than it can make up its mind about anything else. Romantic irony is essentially the intellectual expedient of the subject that keeps its distance from objectivity. We need only ascertain the extent to which the irony of the romantic is directed against himself in practical, thoroughly commonplace reality, and not merely in literary comedies. We can hardly find a person occupied with intellectual matters who would exhibit less self-irony than the typical romantic, Adam Müller. We shall not discover anything even remotely ironic in any of his many letters, in his lectures or speeches, or after a success or a failure. In the case of Friedrich Schlegel, the irony of the objective situation often has such a comical effect that it should not have escaped a herald of irony, who by means of this word continually demanded to be compared with Socrates. The very fact that Friedrich Schlegel is completely lacking in self-irony makes his situation so embarrassing that one prefers to pass over it in silence. The objectification that lies in self-irony, the renunciation of even the last vestiges of subjectivistic illusion, would have endangered the romantic situation. The romantic, as long as he remains a romantic, avoids this instinctively. The target of his irony is clearly not the subject, but rather objective reality, which takes no notice of the subject. Irony is not, however, supposed to destroy reality. On the contrary, retaining the quality of real being, it is supposed to make reality available to the subject as an expedient and make it possible for him to avoid any definitive position. In this way, the claim to the higher and the true reality is not abandoned. Of course the romantic subject could not hold out in this equivocal position for long. In Hegel, who executed romanticism, the state and the world spirit have already become the subjects of the superior irony and intrigue, and they make even the most genial ego into a victim of their irony.

Reality and totality

The result of subjectivistic reserve was that the romantic could not find the reality he sought in himself, the community, the development of world history, or — as long as he remained a romantic — in the God of traditional metaphysics. Yet the longing for reality demanded a fulfillment. With the help of irony, he could protect himself against the sole reality. Nevertheless, irony was nothing more than a weapon with which the subject defended itself. Reality itself was not to be gained in a subjectivistic fashion. In consequence, something else was substituted for it, something apparently even more vast: totality. The subject could make itself master of the entire universe, the totality of science, and the totality of art, all at once and completely. This device was taken from the arsenal of the philosophy of nature. The philosophical construct is also present where it is not romantic — as in J. J. Wagner, where it appears to be the emanation of an unchecked need for a construct that unfolds without any interest in empirical reality. It is not the geometric line, but rather the arabesque that is romantic. The entire philosophy of nature of the Renaissance that developed prior to the great turning point of Descartes has nothing romantic about it. No doubt Schelling's philosophy of nature does, but not as philosophy of nature. Like mystical, theological, philosophical, and other intellectual data, it is put to a romantic use. Like historical and psychological constructs, the constructs of the philosophy of nature are romanticized. This takes place in the most varied forms. The superficial similarity between these forms and other nonromantic processes has led to an immeasurable extension of the word. That is because people cannot free themselves from the idea of regarding everything that interests a romantic and stimulates romantic productivity as being itself essentially romantic as well.

When romantics keep diaries, write letters, analyze, discuss, venerate, and characterize themselves and others, then of course this also lies in the direction of the two new realities: community and history. The romantics transform every thought into a sociable conversation and every instant into a historical moment. They linger over every second and every cadence, and they find this interesting. But they do even more than this. Every moment is transformed into a point in a structure. And just as the romantic emotion moves between the compressed ego and expansion into the cosmos, so every point is a circle at the same time, and every circle a point. The community is an extended individual, the individual a concentrated community. Every historical moment is an elastic point in the vast fantasy of the philosophy of history with which we dispose over peoples and eons. That is the way to guarantee the romantic supremacy over reality. "All the accidents of our life are materials of which we can make whatever we want." Everything is "the first term in an infinite series, the beginning of an endless novel" (Novalis). Here the word *romantic* once more becomes true to its etymological sense: Reality is punctuated, and every point becomes the beginning point for a novel.

What is perceived as romantic rationalism and intellectualism is this ironic deflation of the reality of the world into a fanciful construction. In this way, the two new realities — humanity and history — also became figures that could be "manipulated." There is no self-objectification in the self-aggrandizement of the romantics, no more than their social philosophy contains a political idea or their historical constructions exhibit a sense of history. In everything — their diaries, letters, conversations, sociability, and their occupation with history — they are, in fact, always occupied with themselves. It is almost comical that serious historians regard romanticism as the originator of the historical sense — a movement whose typical expressions include Bettina von Arnim's epistolary novels, which at most can evoke the need for historical authenticity as a response to their amusing nonchalance in the shaping of legends. In the romantic, everything — society and history, the cosmos and humanity — serves only the productivity of the romantic ego. Rousseau says of himself: "But what shall I play with when I am alone at last? With myself. With the entire universe." In a letter to Gentz from the year 1805, Adam Müller explains his occupation with astrology as "intercourse with nature in the high style." Around the same time, he confirms that the reason for his psychic confusion lies in "an all-too-unbridled intercourse with himself." This is it. For the romantic, intercourse with nature is actually intercourse with himself. Neither the cosmos, nor the state, nor the people, nor historical development has any intrinsic interest for him. Everything can be made into an easily managed figuration of the subject that is occupied with itself. The attempt of Schelling's philosophy of nature to surmount the opposition of concept and life by means of a philosophy of identity at least had been cast in a grand intellectual system. The romantics used his formulations without any regard for the system. The reproach that Schelling made against Fichte — that he annihilated nature — became a true frenzy of destruction among the romantics, who made use of Schelling's terms. Everything is reduced to the point. Definition, which the romantics rejected so completely because it comprises a limitation and a restriction, becomes a punctuation without substance. Spirit is . . . Religion is . . . Virtue is . . . Science is . . . Meaning is . . . The animal is . . . The plant is . . . Wit is . . . Charm is . . . The transcendental is . . . The naive is . . . Irony is . . . The impulse to reduce every object to a point is intensified in the innumerable explanations of things as being "nothing other than." They do not include specially emphasized conceptual limitations. On the contrary, they are apodictic identifications that crystallize the point. Here Adam Müller outdoes all the others. The most sublime beauty is nothing other than . . . Art is nothing other than . . . Money is nothing other than . . . Popularity is nothing other than . . . The separation of ideal and reality is nothing other than . . . Positive and negative are nothing other than . . . The entire world is nothing other than nothing else (thus the romantic also had the possibility of providing explanations in terms of the crudest sensualism: the world, therefore, is what it is). Once again, the point is nothing but a concentration of the circle, the circle an expansion of the point. Substantial reality was superseded. The concept was also superseded, and thus this entire game of punctuation and seriation no longer has any relations with analysis and synthesis, and with atomistic and dynamic thought.

The romantic treatment of the universe

The instant, the dreaded second, is also transformed into a point. The present is nothing other than the punctual boundary between past and future. It connects both "by means of limitation." It is "ossification, crystallization" (Novalis). A circle can be wrapped around it as the center. It can also be the point at which the tangent of infinity is contiguous with the circle of the finite. It is also, however, the point of departure for a line into the infinite that can extend in any direction. Thus every event is transformed into a fantastic and dreamlike ambiguity, and every object can become anything. The "universe is the elongation of my beloved." Conversely, "the beloved is the abbreviation of the universe." "Every individual is the center of a system of emanation." Instead of mystical forces, the emanations are geometric lines. The world is resolved into figures, and the purpose is "the manipulation of the universe."[11] Forms without substance can be related to any content. In the romantic anarchy, everyone can form his own world, elevate every word and every sound to a vessel of infinite possibilities, and transform every situation and every event in a romantic fashion, just as Bettina von Arnim does in her epistolary novels. If Novalis says that he believes in the forms of bread and wine in Communion, then we should not ascribe to him a belief different from the one he himself has: Namely, he thinks that everything can be bread and wine. He believes in the Bible; but every authentic book is a Bible. He believes in genius; but every person is a genius. He believes in the Germans; but there are Germans everywhere. In spite of the alleged historical sensitivity of romanticism, for him the German character is not limited to a state and a race. It is not even limited to Germany. The French, in particular, are said to have received a portion of the German character as a result of the revolution of 1789. He glorifies classical antiquity; but classical antiquity is wherever that true spirit can be found. He declares himself to be a royalist and a monarchist; but "every person should be able to assume the throne." He loves only his wife; but with the aid of his imagination he can transform her into thousands of other women.

If this general disintegration, this playful sorcery of the imagination, remained in its own sphere, it would be irrefutable within the confines of its orbit. But it intermixes with the world of commonplace reality in a capricious and arbitrary fashion. In a general exchange and confusion of concepts, an enormous promiscuity of words, everything becomes explicable and inexplicable, identical and antithetical, and everything can be substituted for everything else. Art was applied to questions and discussions of political reality "to transform everything into the beloved Sophie and vice versa."* This general "and vice versa" is the philosopher's stone in the grand alchemy of words that can transform every piece of muck into gold and every piece of gold into muck. Every concept is an ego, and vice versa. Every ego is a concept, every system an individual, and every individual a system. The state is the beloved and becomes a person. The person becomes the state. Or in Müller's *Lehre*

---

*[Tr.] *Alles in Sophien zu verwandeln und umgekehrt.* Sofie is Sophie von Kühn (1782–1797). Novalis met the twelve-year-old Sophie in 1794 and immediately fell in love with her. Shortly after their engagement, she became ill and failed to survive several unsuccessful operations.

vom Gegensatz: If positive and negative are antitheses like object and subject, then positive and negative are nothing but object and subject. They are also, however, space and time, nature and art, science and religion, monarchy and republic, nobility and bourgeoisie, husband and wife, speaker and listener. It is the formula through which "the entire world can pass," in terms of which "the world can be exhaustively disposed," and with which "the universe is demonstrated."

Of course. Only this is not the world and the universe, but rather a small figure of art. The will to reality ended in the will to appearance. The romantics had attempted to grasp the reality of the world, the entire world at once, the totality of the cosmos. Instead they obtained projections and reabsorptions, elongations and abbreviations. The point, the circle, ellipses, and arabesques, an ensouled — that is, a subjectified — cosmic game. They managed to escape the reality of things, and in turn things had also escaped them. When we see them in their writings, letters, and diaries engaged with the manipulation of the universe, they sometimes remind us of the damned in Swedenborg's hell for those who are all-too-cunning. They sit in a cramped barrel, see marvelous figures above them that they take to be the world, and believe that it would be up to them to govern this world.

The occasionalist structure of romanticism

The disillusionment of subjectivism

The reality whose power was actually demonstrated every day remained in obscurity as an irrational quantity. Ontological thought no longer existed. The entire century that was influenced by the romantic spirit is permeated by a characteristic mood. Regardless of how diverse, systematic, and emotional the presuppositions, results, and methods are, above and beyond the difference between optimism and pessimism the anxiety of the single individual and his sense of being deceived can be overheard. We are helpless in the hands of a power that plays with us. We enjoy playing ironically with human beings and the world. It is exciting to imagine that man, like

Prospero in Shakespeare's *The Tempest,* holds the "mechanical play" of the drama in his hands, and romantics are fond of imagining such ideas of an invisible power of free subjectivity. At the end of the eighteenth century and later as well, fantasies about the power of secret alliances were not merely a requisite for cheap thrillers. Their belief in mysterious intrigues on the part of Jesuits, Illuminati, and Freemasons were also manifested by unromantic temperaments of this century. In the idea of a secret power exercised "behind the scenes," concentrated in the hands of a small number of people, and enabling them to control human history invisibly and with supreme malice — in such constructs of the "secret," a rationalistic belief in the conscious domination of historical events by man is combined with a demonic-fanciful fear of an immense social power, and frequently with the secularized belief in providence as well. Here the romantic saw a theme for his ironic and scheming craving for reality: the delight in secret, irresponsible, and frivolous power over human beings.

Thus in Tieck's early novels, there are superior persons who make others into the unconscious tools of their will and intrigue. They experiment as "great engineers in the background of the whole," and they hold the threads of the game in their hands. In the final analysis, however, they are obliged to realize that "in its way, fate plays with us as well . . . a vast game, a farce in which terrible forms are strangely combined in a confused way." Lovell, who had believed that he ruled over the fate of his acquaintances with an ironic superiority, had himself been the tool of the irony of Andrea. And the irony of Andrea again reaches its peak and ends in the utterance: "So what am I? Who is the being so earnestly holding the pen here without tiring of writing down words? In the end, I don't know what I'm doing either. I was very happy to be the chief of a secret and invisible band of robbers, making fools of the entire world. Now the question occurs to me, whether I have not made myself into the greatest fool with this endeavor. . . . Who is the strange self that wrangles with me in this way?"

What did not yet emerge so clearly in Schelling's philosophy as in Luden's philosophy of history, which it influenced, is already as self-evident as a moral in Hegel: The individual human being is an instrument of the reason that evolves in the dialectical process. An unconscious and higher necessity hovers over the freedom of the individual human being. Transcending the conscious will of the individual, history realizes itself involuntarily (Schelling). Persons, peoples, and generations are nothing but necessary tools that the spirit of life requires in order to temporally manifest itself in them and by means of them (Luden). Peoples are instruments of that world spirit. They stand at its throne as the agents of its realization and the witnesses of its splendor. The individual becomes the victim of the "cunning of reason." His understanding and what he conceives with it is "deception" (Hegel). Or human beings and classes are simultaneously tools and consequences of the vast process of production in whose relations they are impelled, above and beyond their calculations (Marx). Or an unconscious, enigmatic, oppressed will directs at its own expense the entire tragedy and comedy of the world with all its details and events, and it treats itself as a spectator at the same time. Thus "life is a continual deception" (Schopenhauer).

In consequence, the truth never lies in what the individual person comprehends or wants because everything is the function of a reality that acts beyond him. The optimism of Hegel and of J. J. Wagner, who is much more naive, lies in the fact that they do not perceive this as a reason for anxiety. Because of their philosophical knowledge, they believe themselves to be members, or at least initiates, of the authoritative tribunal. For them as well, the *true* reason remains different from the manifest reason that the individual person is aware of. It is the effect of a foreign and higher power, however, a power that functions according to a conscious, nomological order. Such a power must necessarily maintain either consciousness or nomological order. That the world spirit is nothing but conscious, logical, nomological order in Hegel's work could be explained on the basis of his panlogistic method. But in Schopenhauer too, the unconscious will that regards itself as a spectator in the drama of the world becomes a romantic subject projected into cosmic dimensions. That happens because, in reality, this will alone is active and — all opposing metaphysical presuppositions notwithstanding — conscious and nomological. In the

Marxist philosophy of history, the forces of production appear as authoritative powers that function in a nomological fashion, and can even produce their own scientific explanation. And in modern psychoanalytical investigations of unconscious psychic processes, the dialectic is repeated with the greatest clarity: A person's dreams as well as other apparently harmless and accidental forms of subconscious activity have the most deliberate and purposeful mechanics, which the "truly" operative force makes use of for its own purposes.

Once again, the two modern demiurges — humanity and history — are active everywhere. The individual person becomes the tool of his sociological surroundings, or the tool of the world spirit that evolves in a world-historical fashion, or the tool of the most diverse combinations of these two factors. This need not lead to a fatalistic or quietistic suspension of human activity. That is because the individual can believe he is a member of his people and can make a contribution in his place. Even in so active and positive a person as de Maistre, the conception prevails — and not as a purely theoretical construct, but rather in an emotionally authentic fashion — that every person is only the tool of God. In de Maistre, however, we already find signs of the extent to which the feeling of dependence on God is connected with the feeling of dependence on the national community and its historical development. As a result, the conflation of the two did not amount to an additional step. Citing Plutarch and accepting the traditional classical view, he calls the body a tool of the soul. In the same way, the soul is a tool of God. The person then grows in his national community like an acorn in its soil, and he imagines that, in spite of this, he could do something. And yet he is only the "trowel that imagines it is the master builder." The aversion that Burke, de Maistre, and Bonald have for "artifice" in political affairs, artificial constitutions based on the calculations of a clever individual, and the fabricators of constitutions and political geometricians arises from the feeling that the basis of all historical-political events lies in a superindividual power — where *basis* in their work signifies both causal explanation and normative justification or legitimation. The romantics, who blended these ideas with their subjectivistic constructs of the world, were fond of perceiving themselves as members of a higher organism. "Dancing, eating, speaking, communal feeling and working, being together, seeing, feeling, and listening to oneself, and so on — these are all conditions and occasions, even functions of the agency of a higher, composite human being, the genius" (Novalis). Just as in the schism between reality and possibility and between finitude and infinity, the community and history had availed themselves of functions that, in Christian metaphysics, belonged to God, here too they became the true cause for which everything else is only an *occasion*. Closer examination shows, however, that it is neither of these two demiurges — humanity and history — but rather the romantic subject itself that takes everything as an occasion. Here the opposition of romantic productivity to the activity that Fichte's "ego" postulates is the appropriate point of departure for the exposition of the romantic character. That is because this Fichtean "ego" became the romantic subject.

The meaning of *occasio* as the antithesis of *causa*: the occasional as the relation of the subjectivistic and the fanciful

In Fichte, the world, the "nonego," becomes matter that must be worked upon. It is to be transformed in "absolute causality" and absolute activity. In this way, however, intervention in the mechanism of the causal relations of external reality becomes necessary, and a calculable nexus — in other words, one that is adequate in terms of the relationship between cause and effect — must be supposed. As early as 1801, Hegel, with an unerring sense of genius, had already recognized that the connection with the rationalism of the previous century, and thus the historical inadequacy of the system, lay in the causal relationship between the ego and the nonego. The romantics were incapable of this sort of philosophical insight. On the contrary, they were still completely under the spell of Fichte's intellectual dominance. Schleiermacher at least sensed the opposition and (in the *Athenaeum*) pointed it out. This mastery of the world was too mechanical and technical for him. In any case, this is the decisive point. Namely, if anything provides a complete definition of romanticism, it is the lack of any relationship to a *causa*. Not only does it resist absolute causality — in other words, an absolutely calculable and adequate relationship of *cause and effect* such as the science of mechanics must presuppose; the relationship between *stimulus and response* that prevails in the sciences of organic life remains calculable within certain limits as well. In the sense of an "action" or a "cause," the word *causa* also has the meaning of a teleological or normative bond and an intellectual or moral force that admits an adequate relation. On the other hand, an absolutely inadequate relationship obtains between *occasio and effect*. Since any concrete item can be the *occasio* of an incalculable effect — for Mozart, a look at an orange can be the occasion for composing the duet *Là ci darem la mano* — this relationship is completely incommensurable, devoid of all objectivity, and nonrational. It is the relation of the fanciful.

How is it possible for this relation to transform the world? Novalis provides the answer: "All the accidents of our life are materials from which we can make whatever we want. Everything is the first member of an infinite series (up to this point, the sentence could still articulate a magical mysticism, but the conclusion is a manifestation of romanticism:), the beginning of an endless novel." This fragment (number 66) provides the real formula of the romantic. The fact that it is not accidental (which, naturally, holds true for much that is in Novalis and in all romanticism) is shown in the other fragment by Novalis about Goethe (number 29). Goethe has the ability to connect small and insignificant occurrences with important events. Life is full of such accidents. "They constitute a game that, like all play, comes down to surprise and deception." According to Novalis, the conversation as well — this darling concept of romanticism — is a "verbal game," and according to Friedrich Schlegel, its theme is only a "vehicle" for the delight taken in the conversation. In particular, the arbitrary alteration of reality in Bettina von Arnim's epistolary novels is a splendid example of romantic praxis. Every interesting encounter becomes the occasion for a novel. Thus in the romantic, it also turns out that there is a transformation of the world, but a different one from the one Fichte had postulated. It was transformation in play and the imagination, "poeticizing": in other words, the use of what is concretely given, even each sense perception, as the occasion for a "fable," a poem, an object of aesthetic sensation, or — because this best conforms to the etymology of the word *romanticism* — a novel [*Roman*]. This explains the following apparently complicated romantic phenomena: Fichte's absolute ego, revamped in an emotional and aestheticized fashion, results in an altered world, not by means of activity, but by mood and imagination.

Romantic productivity consciously rejects every connection to a *causa,* and thus also every activity that intervenes in the real connections of the visible world. And yet, like Fichte's ego, it can be absolutely creative in absolute subjectivity, namely, by producing chimeras, by "poeticizing." So in order to apprehend its nature, we should not do what has generally been done thus far: begin with the romanticized object (with the Middle Ages or old castles) instead of with the romanticizing subject; or, in Shaftesbury's terminology, we should not begin with the "Beautifyed" instead of with the "Beautifying." For the romantic achievement, the external world and historical reality are of interest only insofar as they can be — to use that expression from Novalis — the beginning of a novel. The given fact is not objectively considered in a political, historical, legal, or moral context. On the contrary, it is the object of an aesthetic and emotional interest, something with which the romantic enthusiasm catches fire. For a productivity of this sort, what it depends upon lies so completely in the domain of the subjective, in what the romantic ego adds from itself, that, correctly considered, we can no longer speak of an object. This is because the object becomes the mere "occasion," the "beginning," the "elastic point," "incitement," "vehicle," or however the paraphrases of *occasio* by the romantics should be read. As Friedrich Schlegel wrote to his brother in 1791,[12] everything of a more elevated character that we find in the beloved is our own work. The beloved deserves no credit for it. "The beloved was only the occasion," as it is put in *Lucinde,* only the "marvelous flower of your imagination." Surrender to this romantic productivity involves the conscious renunciation of an adequate relationship to the visible, external world. Everything real is only an occasion. The object is without substance, essence, and function. It

is a concrete point about which the romantic game of fantasy
moves. As a starting point, this concrete point always remains
present, but without any commensurable relation to the romantic digression, which is the only thing essential. In consequence, there is no possibility of distinguishing a romantic
object from the other object — the queen, the state, the beloved, the Madonna — precisely because there are no longer
any objects, but only *occasiones*.

The nature of the old occasionalism: the suspension of
antitheses by means of a higher third factor

In the history of philosophy, the concept of *occasio* found its
place in the systems of so-called occasionalism, in Géraud de
Cordemoy, Geulincx, and Malebranche. The name is justified
to the extent that these systems place the *occasio*, in opposition
to the *causa*, at a decisive point in their metaphysical construct,
usually, of course, without a more precise definition of the
concept of *occasion*. Malebranche, for example, even speaks of
causes occasionneles, and in this way muddles his entire system,
which justified his contemporaries in reproaching him for a
fundamental confusion. Nevertheless, that this most singular
concept appears here in opposition to *causa* remains of decisive
importance. That is because it marked the appearance of a
new and special type of metaphysical attitude, even if at the
outset this did not happen with the complete abandon and
disintegration that are implicit in the idea of the occasional. In
the philosophers just mentioned, God — in the sense of traditional Christian metaphysics — is retained. In their works,
therefore, the distinctive qualities of the occasionalist attitude
toward the world are exhibited only indirectly. This is because,
although the world and what occurs in it are indeed only an
occasion, they are an occasion for God, in which order and law
are recovered.

   The problem of the true cause is the initial problem of
occasionalism. It found every true cause in God and explained
all the events of this world as a mere occasion. Here again we
see the justification of the view that the discussion of the structure of the romantic spirit began with Descartes, who was led

from the argument that I exist because I think — from the inference from thought to being — to the distinction between internal and external, soul and body, *res cogitans* and *res extensa*. This resulted in the logical and metaphysical difficulties of bringing the two into interaction with one another and of explaining the mutual interaction of soul and body. The occasionalistic solution undertaken in the systems of Géraud de Cordemoy, Geulincx, and Malebranche eliminated the difficulties by regarding God as the true cause of every single psychic and physical event. God brings about the inexplicable correspondence of mental and corporeal phenomena. Everything taken together — the conscious process, the volitional impulse, and the muscular movement — is a mere occasion for God's activity. In fact, it is not the human being who acts, but rather God. Cordemoy claims that *nihil facimus nisi auxilio potentiae quae nostra non est* [we do not act except by the aid of a power that is not our own]; and by this he means the natural event, not the effects of grace. In every single case, God's intervention is the real efficacy, the *efficacité propre*.

The occasionalists find paraphrases and comparisons for this process that often call to mind romantic dispositions. When I build a house, it is a higher power that forms my plan, guides my hand, and moves every stone so that, finally, a house results. *Spectator sum in hac scena, non actor* [I am a spectator in this scene, not an actor] (Geulincx). We could also mention here the frequently cited example of the writing pen, which reappears in the passage from Tieck's *Lovell* that was just noted. When I write, God moves the pen. He moves my hand and my will, which sets my hand in motion. Writing is really a movement of God. *Quando homo movet calamum, homo nequaquam illum movet, sed motus calami est accidens a Deo in calamo creatus* [When a man moves the pen, it is not he who moves it at all. Rather the movement of the pen is an accidental property of the pen created by God]. And yet in spite of the frequent romantic use of such motifs, the general distinction between appearance and essence and the mystical undermining of palpable reality would not be able to establish a specific connection with the romantic spirit. Although it is indeed significant, it is still not decisive that in spite of his apparent rationalism, imagination is really dominant in the case of Malebranche, who was regarded as a "dreamer." Sainte-Beuve in particular has noticed this, with brilliant psychological observations.[13] Further, it is important that Malebranche vehemently opposed typical classical figures, Seneca and Cato, and the Stoic ideal of the wise man.[14] In light of Dilthey's demonstration of the comprehensive significance of the Stoic tradition for the seventeenth and eighteenth centuries, such an attack should no longer be overlooked. Finally, Malebranche was a source — unknown to most people, but for all that no less abundant — for an eighteenth-century author who constituted a counterweight to the abstract rationalism of the French Enlightenment: for Montesquieu, and especially for his theory of the climatic and geographical distinctiveness of the human spirit. On this point, Montesquieu's remark about Tertullian is an astonishing example.[15] Nevertheless, the decisive point lies in the structural distinctiveness of occasionalism.

This distinctiveness rests on the consideration that the occasionalist does not clear up a dualism, but rather lets it stand. He makes it illusory, however, by shifting into a comprehensive third sphere. If every psychic and physical process appears only as an action of God, then the difficulty contained in the supposition of an interaction between soul and body is not solved on the basis of this supposition, and the question is not resolved. The interest simply slips from a dualistic result into a more general, "higher," and "true" unity. To a person who believes in God, this does not at all seem a superficial solution brought about by a *deus ex machina*. Perhaps he will experience it as "organic" in the highest degree. This is because, for him, there is no dualism in what is essential, in God. The God of the occasionalistic system essentially has this function of being true reality, in which the opposition between body and soul disappears into the domain of the unreal. This God is somewhat different from Schelling's absolute indifference. As long as thought moves in a cyclical fashion, it is not occasionalistic. That is because it does not leave the orbit of oppositions. But as soon as the "organism" is not merely polarized in oppositions — as in the romantics, when their ideas are not obliterated by suggestions that stem from Schelling — a "higher third" factor suspends the oppositions, and in such a way that the antithetically grouped things disappear into the "higher third" and the opposition becomes the occasion for this "higher third." The opposition between the sexes is suspended in the "total human being"; the opposition between individuals in the higher organism, the "state," or the people; the discord between states in the higher organization, the Church. Whatever has the power to employ the opposition as the occasion for its higher and exclusive efficacy is the true and higher reality.

The romantic suspension of antitheses by means of another higher factor: true reality and the different claimants to this reality (the ego, the people, history, God)

This also holds true for Adam Müller, who is always fond of talking about mediation and interaction. Insofar as something in his work can be discerned in the motley combination of elements from Schelling, Schlegel, and numerous other sources, it is the following. He had begun with a theory of polarity that explicitly rejected an absolute identity as a "celebrated misconception," and he proclaimed a kind of "antithetical synthesis" as the ultimate principle: namely, antithesis. Each thing is nothing but its antithesis. Nature is antiart. Art is antinature. The flower is the antithesis of the antiflower. And ultimately, the antithesis itself depends upon the anti-antithesis. In the first place, the old liberal idea of balance, as it appears in Burke and Shaftesbury, is still easily recognizable here. At the same time, however, Müller says that the antitheses cannot be overcome by means of a "mechanical" interaction. It is supposed to happen by means of a higher factor, the "idea." He always stressed that the idea of humanity employed two human beings for its realization, a man and a woman. Along the same lines, he says that every contract presupposes two parties — but in addition, a common third factor, a basis that comprehends both. The opposition that he repeatedly discovers in reality is often simply balanced in the old liberal fashion.[16] Often, however, it appears as the emanation of a higher identity. It was precisely in such trains of thought that the new world view saw its superiority over the lifeless analytical rationalism of the previous century and the "mechanistic" doctrine of equilibrium. In this context, however, the idea of emanation is not the primary consideration. The point of departure was the antithetical quality of what is concretely present and real, a quality that must be suspended. Its suspension takes place in such a way that a higher third factor (first the idea, then the state, and finally God) takes the antitheses as the occasion for its higher power. In this regard, a twofold consideration should be noted. First, the train of thought always begins with a concrete antithesis and proceeds to another concrete factor (the higher third factor); moreover, the antithetically grouped concrete things are always merely the bearers of a mediation on the part of the higher mediating power, which manifests itself on the occasion of the antithesis. Just as Malebranche speaks of "communication" as the real force, so Adam Müller speaks of "mediation." For the romantics, everything is accounted for by virtue of the fact that, in this way, the concrete antithesis and heterogeneity disappear in a higher factor. The community, for example, can play the role of the higher third factor. In that case, everything is conceived in terms of "sociability" or "association." Wit is logical sociability. Mind is logical sociability. Money is nothing but sociability. From the standpoint of romanticism, however, the community is never the product of individual factors. The individual factors are instead "occasions or even functions" of the community. Here we also see the general tendency in the direction of the "higher third" factor, the true reality.

When romantics return to the God of Christian metaphysics, this structure of the romantic spirit clearly stands out. In the appendix to his lectures on logic, Friedrich Schlegel mentioned Malebranche with special sympathy and placed him far above Descartes. Later it became clear how much this sympathy of the romantic was based on an identification. Because it explains the move to Catholicism, it is decisive for the concept of romanticism. The entire philosophy of the Catholic Schlegel proceeds from the dilemma: nature and man. Either man (spirit) destroys nature (corporeality), or nature destroys man. For Schlegel, Fichte's idealism and Schelling's philosophy of nature were only special instances of this dilemma. Deliverance came directly from God. That Schlegel, above all, insisted on the positive truth of the Christian religion is explained, first of all, by the consideration that he wanted to deny the errors of his own earlier philosophy of nature. But in addition this insistence includes the ultimately decisive and unconditional recognition of the intervening higher third factor as the true cause.

Adam Müller took over Schlegel's philosophy, often verbatim.[17] But this was not one of the many cases in which he succumbed to the influence of heterogeneous impressions. That is because here it is a matter of the immanent consistency of his own mode of thought. He always had looked for the nature of things in a sphere different from the one to which they belonged, and thus he shifted from one domain to another. For Müller, the nature of money as an economic factor lies in the domain of law, not in the domain of the economy. The nature of the legal does not lie in itself, but rather in the theological. In this way, civil law and constitutional law, which would be qualitative antitheses in the domain of the legal, were supposed to become imaginary, or at most purely quantitative, distinctions. In *Ueber die Notwendigkeit einer theologischen Grundlage der gesamten Staatswissenschaften* [On the necessity of a theological basis for the political sciences], this is the sense of his entire account. The human being cannot take a single step without a chasm opening. In consequence, even the endless conflict between legitimists and liberals can be put right only by divine intervention. God alone puts history in motion. Müller uses this point politically, in order to pose a simple objection to the liberal claims of peoples who appeal to their great sacrifices and accomplishments in the wars of independence: The great successes, the defeat of Napoleon, were the work of God, not of men. Thus the populace cannot derive any political demands from this consideration. Earlier, when he was still under the influence of the philosophy of nature, he would have said that these successes were the work of the "vital energy" of the nation, produced solely in the opposition between prince and people,[18] or the result of organic historical growth. That is because great things of this sort could not have been "fabricated" by human beings. Except when Müller was concerned with the apologetics of everyday political affairs, his

main point was always that the antithetical quality of the concrete event redeems the sole true efficacy of the sole true
reality.

The result: whatever happens to be different as the higher
factor; the conflation of concepts

The fact that reserving one's position between several realities
— the ego, the people, the state and history — and playing
them off against one another belongs to the nature of the
romantic situation is confusing, and it conceals the simple structure of its mode of being. An occasionalism with several "true
causes" acting promiscuously could deceive anyone concerning
its true nature. It is an occasionalism that shifts from one reality
to another. For this occasionalism, the "higher third" factor —
which, occasionalistically, necessarily includes something that is
remote, alien, and other — shifts to the other or the alien as
such in the continual deflection to another domain. And finally,
when the traditional idea of God collapses, the other and the
alien become one with the true and the higher. Romanticism
is consummated only under this condition. As long as the
romantic believed that he was himself the transcendental ego,
he did not have to be troubled by the question of the true
cause: he was himself the creator of the world in which he
lived. In the "Grundlage" [Fundamentals] of his *Wissenschaftslehre* [Theory of science], Fichte had recognized that the systematic part of his theory was Spinozism, "except that every
single ego was itself the highest substance," the God of Spinoza's system. Now the world was explained on the basis of the
ego — not, as in Berkeley, as *esse-percepi*, but rather as a creative
act of the ego. The situation of the romantic rests on the
consideration that although he did indeed always reserve for
himself the identification with the creator of the world, he did
not persevere in this position. That is because from the standpoint of the individual empirical subject, it is clearly a fantastical impossibility. In the final analysis, Fichte too had again
made a distinction between the "true" ego and the empirical
ego. In this way, he had again conjured up the old uncertainty
for psychological reality, on which everything depends in this

context. The romantics did not arrive at the identification with the people or with history, and the good conscience of Hegelianism remained alien to them. As a result, they floated from one reality to another: from the ego to the people, the "idea," the state, history, the Church — as long as they remained romantics, always playing off one reality against another and never committing themselves in this game of intrigue that is played with realities. The reality of which the romantics speak always stands in opposition to another reality. The "true" and the "genuine" signify the rejection of the real and the contemporary. Ultimately, it is only what exists in another place and another time, what is absolutely different. As persons who have a concrete existence, they could not regard as realities the constructs from the philosophy of nature and the philosophy of history with which they manipulated the universe. The words they used were without substance because they always spoke only about themselves, not about objects. Solger complained that "one doesn't want to live, but rather to chatter about life." We are repeatedly assured, in empty and fatiguing reiterations, that what is at stake is the "genuine" concept and not the spurious one, the "true," the "real," "genuine" freedom, the "true" revolution, the "genuine" priest, the "true" religiosity, the "true" book, "true" popularity, the "genuine" commercial spirit, the "genuine" republic (the nature of which lies in the fact that it is a "genuine" monarchy), "genuine" jurisprudence, "true" marriage, "true" romanticism, the "true" scholars, the "real" educated classes, "genuine" criticism, and the "true" artists — a list that could easily be continued for many pages. A new concept, however, is not created by prefixing the predicate *genuine* to an old one. After the intoxication of being the creator of the world had lapsed, the following simple reversal took place in a mood of disillusionment. The subject, playing ironically with the world, felt that he was an object of the irony of numerous true realities. The Hegelian spoke of the cunning of reason, but he believed he stood behind the scenes of world history. He knew what was at stake, and either he had outfoxed the cunning of world history, or he was legitimately engaged on the side of true reason. The romantic, on the other hand, was immediately in a state of despair, for in him several realities were ironically at play in a confused fashion.

Romantic productivity: the world as the occasion for an experience; the essentially aesthetic mode of this productivity

One should have thought that this state would have destroyed a person intellectually — assuming that his life served interests that were exclusively intellectual — and physically as well. Instead, romanticism as a total phenomenon ended in the Biedermeier, perhaps not a disgraceful end, but not a tragic one either. Revolutionary inner strife became an idyll. The bourgeois was in rapture over romanticism and saw in it his artistic ideal and his rejuvenation. The cycle of antitheses from revolution to idyll was ended. The ironic romantic had become the victim of an evil irony. In the *Athenaeum*, Schlegel had proclaimed that the all-embracing, transcendental poetry of romanticism begins as satire, is suspended as elegy in its middle period, and ends as idyll with the absolute identity of the ideal and the real. And this is also what happened. It is a romantic error to call the idyll of the Dresden Lyric Circle, that clique of philistine dilettantes, pseudoromanticism. It was the consummation of romanticism. Consider also the Austrian Biedermeier, about which the intelligent and earnest Jarcke complained that it was "a melodious but hollow and dissolute poetry, unchristian in its innermost nature, enfeebling the dialectical powers of scholars, and dulling the moral instinct." This philistine idyll also belongs to romanticism. Romanticism had begun with satires against the philistine. In the philistine, it beheld insipid and base reality, the antithesis of the true, higher reality that it sought. The romantic hated the philistine. But it turned out that the philistine loved the romantic, and in such a relationship it was obvious that the philistine had the dominant position.

The conflict of realities had not really torn the romantic to pieces. It had affected him. It was a conflict in which the romantic took no active part, because all he thought about was maintaining himself with his subjectivity. He had observed a conflict and was deeply moved by the sensation. Malebranche defined human beings as created spirits: substances that perceive that they are affected or altered. If we disregard the pre-Kantian concept of substance, that could be a definition of the romantic. In other words, the problem of occasionalism is not merely metaphysical; it is just as much an ethical problem. It concerns the ancient question of human free will: the question of the status and content of human activity. Of course the romantic, under the illusion of Fichte's *Wissenschaftslehre*, did, *eo ipso*, everything. He was responsible only to his autonomous ego. But in practice, everything and nothing are really identities in such cases, and the question remains: What does human activity consist in? According to the ethic of the systems of occasionalism, it is only an emotion. A moral act is an act of evaluation. The person accompanies the act of another person with his assent or rejection, with an affirmative or negative judgment. His freedom consists in "assent," in a feeling of value, a judgment, and a criticism. It is precisely the ethics of rationalistic systems that favor limiting the person to "assenting" to the immutable nomological necessity of the event. In romanticism, however, this idea also is sentimentalized and deformed in an emotive direction. This also begins as early as Malebranche. God creates and produces. The human being follows the event with his feelings. In this way, however, he participates in the process. Where true reality was clearly and unambiguously perceived, as in Malebranche — who has to be considered a sincere Catholic Christian, even though he himself saw the death of Christ as a mere *occasio* for salvation — the impression of being an *occasio* in the hand of God did not exclude a consciousness of responsibility. Human beings, who are firmly rooted in their religious, social, and national milieu, belong to the community that grows around them and with which they themselves grow. It is different when occasionalism is subjectified: in other words, when the isolated subject treats the world as an *occasio*. In that case, the activity of the subject consists only in the fanciful animation of its affect. The romantic reacts only with his affect. His activity is the affective echo of an activity that is necessarily not his own.

The distinctive quality of the intellectual type that can be characterized as occasionalistic lies, first of all, in the following consideration: Instead of offering the solution to the problem, he provides a resolution of the factors of the problem. It was asked how body and soul can interact. The answer: The action of the body and the soul does not matter because both are merged in the infinite and comprehensive third factor, in God, the only thing that acts. This answer is merely a manifestation of the essential and more profound basic tendency of that type. The occasionalist, for whom the world is suspended in God, does not really think pantheistically, but rather panentheistically. In that case, all activity seems to be concentrated in God, and whatever there is in the way of deserving activity is a gift of God's grace. In Adam Müller, the following thesis provides a clear example of this panentheism transposed from God to the state.[19] Everywhere and at all times, man "without the state cannot hear, see, think, feel, or love. He can be conceived only as *in the state.*" If the occasionalistic concept of God is examined more closely, however, the activity of God becomes problematic too. In Descartes, God is absolute volition, which does whatever it wants with an unconditionally free will. Malebranche, on the other hand, as just mentioned, makes God into a general order that occurs in complete harmony and in which even the efficacy of grace follows in a nomological fashion. The fundamental aversion to all personal activity and efficacy leads consistently to an idea of God in which the personality of God is nullified. Descartes sees the basis of moral laws in the will of God. For Malebranche, moral laws constitute an eternal order in which not even God can alter anything. Malebranche, of course, abhorred Spinoza's pantheism and protested against it on the grounds that it placed truth or nomological necessity above even the personal God. He also charged Spinoza with atheism. But Malebranche himself cannot escape the result that the personal God is transformed into a general order of nature. In Malebranche, the generality of the idea of "order" is only apparently a case of Cartesian rationalism. In fact, it signifies the dissolution of the activity of God into a general harmony. Why did Christ found a church? The order wants it this way. Why are devout prayers answered? The order wants them to be carried out. Why is the sinner not granted a favorable hearing? The order does not desire it. Such arguments were based on a conviction that the orthodox perceived as ungodly. How does it happen, Fénelon asked, that the philosophers want to limit God's authority? It is true that in this way God is subjected to a general order, and that the authoritative command and all activity become impossible. Here there is an analogy with the thinking of political revolutionaries who attempted to subject the monarch to the general will. It is the ancient opposition for which Tertullian found the classical formulation: *audaciam existimo de bono divi praecepti disputare, neque enim quia bonum est, idcirco auscultare debemus, sed quia deus praecipit* [I consider it presumptuous to debate the goodness of a divine precept. We should attend to it, not because it is good, but because God has prescribed it]. As a result, Malebranche also was exposed as an atheist, and the Jesuit Hardouin admitted him along with Descartes, Pascal, and others into the catalog of his "exposed atheists." Sainte-Beuve characterized Father Hardouin as a fool because he called Pascal an atheist. He was not a fool, but only a rabid pedagogue with a vast erudition. The German romantics Schlegel and Müller, however, called their own past atheistic, and whoever is fond of slogans could reduce their development to the epigram: Malebranche, who is converted to Father Hardouin.

This conception does not arise from an abstract sense of right — not, as in Kant, from a juridical structure of thought. Even in the most extreme case, the occasionalist would not be a pedant or a legalistic tyrant. He will not act, and even less will he enforce something. Just as he dodges the initial problem — the interaction of body and soul — it is essential to him that he avoid every concrete reality and efficacy as well, that he make every earthly and finite efficacy into the *occasio* for the one and only essential efficacy, and that he assign to himself only assent — and here that means an attendant mood. This is exhibited even more conspicuously in romanticism, where the concept of the *occasio* develops its full disintegrative power. That is because now it is no longer God, something absolute and objective, that stands in the center. On the contrary, the individual subject treats the world as the *occasio* of his activity and productivity. For him, even the greatest external event — a revolution or a world war — is intrinsically indifferent. The

incident becomes significant only when it has become the occasion for a great experience, a genial apprehension, or some
other romantic creation. Therefore true reality has only what
the subject makes into the object of its creative interest. By
means of a simple reversal, the subject has become the creator
of the world. It designates as the world only what served it as
the occasion of an experience. Here a colossal consciousness of
personality seems to be concentrated in colossal activity. Nevertheless, the amour-propre of the romantic does not change any
of the psychic facts that always hold for the occasionalistic type:
namely, that it has no other activity except that of mood. Of
course this is valued as being higher than "ordinary" activity.
The unbroken subjectivism of early romanticism saw an
achievement even in the impressionistic experience. Affect as
a psychic fact was intrinsically interesting. When it was worked
up into an artistic or logical-systematic artifact, the vital intensity of the experience already seemed to be jeopardized. The
sound of nature was exalted. A sigh, a cry, a summons, "the
kiss that the poeticizing child breathes forth in artless song,"
were already sufficient to qualify as a romantic achievement
and were also perceived as an action by a circle of sympathetic
souls. A friend can make a deeper impression with a sigh than
a stranger can make with the most beautiful poem. Accordingly, if the intensity of subjective impression is all that matters,
the friend's sigh would be the more artistic achievement. Soon,
of course, the necessity of a "gymnastics" of artistic creation
was discovered, and the romantic had to shape his mood or
transcribe it in articulate speech. In other words, he had to
submit to certain aesthetic or logical laws. The romantics who
really had a lyrical talent, for example, certainly did not give
up writing good poems in which mood shifted in a lyrical form.
Herein lay the acknowledgment of a certain "order," which of
course limited itself to the region of the aesthetic. We should
not overlook, however, the point that for the romantic subject
every form of art that it used was also merely an occasion, just
like every concrete point of reality, which served as a point of
departure for the romantic interest. The mood of the subject
was the focal point of this kind of productivity. It remained
both the *terminus a quo* and the *terminus ad quem*, regardless of

whether a lyrical poem, literary criticism, or a philosophical argument was at stake. The object was always nothing more than an occasion.

In this state, it is by no means the case that the external world is negated. Every concrete point of the external world can be the "elastic point": in other words, the beginning of the romantic novel, the *occasio* for the adventure, the point of departure for the fanciful game. Thus the "sensuous coloration" of the romantic, in opposition to the mystic. The romantic, who has no interest in really changing the world, regards it as good if it does not disturb him in his illusion. Irony and intrigue provide him with enough weapons to secure his subjectivistic autarchy and to hold out in the domain of the occasional. For the rest, he leaves external things to their own nomological order. In commonplace reality, the intellectual revolutionary loves external order, even when he theoretically postulates tumult and chaos. As early as Malebranche, who made the *amour de l'ordre* the most important virtue of his ethical system, it must have been conspicuous that he wants to hold on to positive and ecclesiastical Christianity, in spite of his panentheistic rationalism. It is with the greatest intolerance that he judges malefactors who disturb the ecclesiastical order, and it was inconceivable to him that he could come into a real conflict with the external order of the sphere in which he lived. In occasionalism, the aversion to external conflict that is natural among philosophers displays the specific opposition of two polar extremes: the suspension of all reality in God and the recognition of what is positively real as such. The occasionalists experienced the endeavor to do something as a sinful inclination. They analyzed it with psychological subtleties that frequently recall the surprising self-characterizations of the romantics. In his ethics, however, even Geulincx — who discovered the *diabolus ethicus* precisely at this point — unconditionally requires that one fulfill what presents itself to him as a duty in the sphere in which he lives. This is a kind of quietism that can be characterized as legitimist passivity. That is because it again recognized the positively given as such — even though it previously made the positively given insignificant — and because it permits no change in what exists.

The distinctive character of romantic occasionalism is that it subjectifies the main factor of the occasionalist system: God. In the liberal bourgeois world, the detached, isolated, and emancipated individual becomes the middle point, the court of last resort, the absolute. Naturally the illusion of being God could be maintained only in pantheistic or panentheistic sentiments. In psychological reality, therefore, it combined with other, less subjectivistic affects. The subject always claimed, however, that his experience was the only thing of interest. This claim can be realized only in a bourgeois order based on rules. Otherwise the "external conditions" for the undisturbed occupation with one's own mood are not satisfied. Psychologically and historically, romanticism is a product of bourgeois security. One could fail to recognize this only as long as one committed the error of considering as romanticism itself things that happen to be favorite romantic objects, such as chivalry and the Middle Ages — in other words, sundry themes and occasions of the romantic interest. A robber knight can be a romantic figure, but he is not a romantic. The Middle Ages is a powerfully romanticized complex, but it is not romantic. It is only the romanticizing subject and its activity that are of importance for the definition of the concept. It is true that this subject did not romanticize its presupposition, the bourgeois order, but rather preferred to ironize this order because it was the actual present. Concerning Schlegel's ideal state, it has been claimed, and not with injustice, that its locus is not so much the Middle Ages as it is the police state of "German — and at that time, this means petty and pedantic — form."[20] The fact that the genial subject dethroned God was a revolution. But since the romantic remained an occasionalist, it was only an "intellectual" — that is, in fact, an aesthetic — revolution. The revolutionary terminology with which early romanticism appeared on the scene can be explained precisely on the basis of the occasionalist character of romanticism. At that time, the Revolution was the great, impressive event and was sufficiently remote from Germany. Therefore the romantic reacted in conformity with this tendency. The possibility of a real political revolution in which he could personally take part did not occur to him. Regardless of whether his phraseology was revolutionary or reactionary, belligerent or pacifistic, pagan or Christian, he was never resolved to leave the world of his impressionistic experience and change anything that occurred in commonplace reality.

But how does romanticism arrive at that varying acceptance or rejection of any event at all, such as the French Revolution? These are the concomitant emotive states with which the romantic follows historical development. Affirmations and denials, regardless of how much they are stressed in literary, historical, or political criticism, should not be regarded as expressions of resolute activity. That is because in this context, affirmation and denial signify only an antithesis, an opposition. The "antithetical" structure of manifestations of romanticism has a twofold basis, one formal and other material. Words, concepts, and images are formally grouped under the aesthetic perspective of contrast. The significance of this aesthetic factor will be illustrated in the following chapter, especially with reference to Adam Müller's productivity. Here the issue concerns the antithetical quality of the material — the moods and feelings that naturally confront one another as pleasure and aversion, delight and pain, consent and rejection, affirmation and denial, approbation and disgust. But the reaction to a stimulus that stresses pleasure and aversion is not an activity. A person does not become an active personality in the moral sense by feeling pleasure and aversion, regardless of the intensity; nor does this happen when one's condition induces one to make impressive paraphrases. The instances of consent and refusal that we encounter in the reasoning of romantics constitute such paraphrases. That is because they do not mean that the author wants to make up his mind in the usual sense and set to work in the external world. This is something he simply could not do without realizing his unlimited possibilities in a limited reality, without emerging from his subjectivistic creativity and concerning himself with the mechanism of cause and effect or with normative ties. He could not make up his mind without relinquishing his superior irony; in other words, without giving up his romantic situation. The romantic wants to do nothing except experience and paraphrase his experience in an emotionally impressive fashion. This is why, in his case, arguments and inferences become the reverberating figures of his emotional states of affirmation and denial, emotional states that — after they have experienced the liberating and occasional stimulus of an object in the external world — revolve around themselves "in lofty circles."

The blending of intellectual spheres among the intellectualistic romantics

In paraphrasing emotional states of consent and rejection, a distinctive romantic productivity develops, a form of quasi-argumentation that has a special technique. It is natural to paraphrase consent by referring to something that is positive. This is juxtaposed to what is rejected as something that is negative. To begin with, *positive* is used only in the sense of "affirmation." It acquires a special meaning, however, by virtue of the fact that the romantics associate themselves with positive Christianity. Then this meaning is enhanced by a new modification because Haller employs the word in a special way. The positive is the animate. The negative is naturally the lifeless. The animate is organic. The lifeless is mechanical (or also, in Schlegel, dynamic) and anorgic (inorganic). The organic is naturally the genuine. The mechanical is the surrogate, and so on. As a result, the following sequences can easily be compiled from the essays of Friedrich Schlegel and Adam Müller:

Positive	Negative
animate	dynamic-mechanical-mathematical, rigid
organic	inorganic
genuine or true	surrogate (appearance, deception)
persistent	momentary
preserving	destroying
historical	arbitrary
stable	chaotic
peaceful	factious, polemical
legitimate	revolutionary
Christian	pagan
estatist-corporatist	absolutist-centralist

The individual members of these sequences have a particular history. It is evident that *animate* and *organic* belong together. Indeed, this was how romanticism began. Adam Müller brought duration and the moment into the romantic sequence of arguments. Within the positive, a distinction is made between the positive as animate and the positive as a brute fact that is crudely materialistic (Haller is reproached for taking the latter view). In the terminology of early romanticism, "stable" is not really positive. In the year 1820, however, Bonald's concept of *fixité* could not easily be understood other than as positive. Moreover its negative instance is the "rigid," so that it can be differentiated. The concrete relationships to which this schema applies, however, are relatively interchangeable. If only they can be subsumed under one member of a sequence, it is easy to develop the entire sequence and set the entire argument in a powerful motion.

The single members ground and support one another in a reciprocal fashion. For example, if revolution appears as an eruption of new life, it is easy to ascribe the predicates of the positive sequence to it and claim that it was "really" a Christian movement directed against the pagan absolutism of the Enlightenment. On the other hand, when the legitimate appears as the historical and the historical is the organic, then it follows that the legitimate is also the animate. And since the revolutionary is the negation of the legitimate, it must "follow" that the revolutionary is also the purely momentary, the inorganic, the mechanical, the pagan, and, curiously enough, even the rigid. Metternich's police state is undoubtedly legitimate. Therefore it is also Christian, genuine, organic, and animate. And if it understood itself correctly, it would have to become estatist and corporatist. If someone wanted to proceed from the assumption that this kind of state can be called absolutist, however, then he would easily prove the contrary: that it is actually revolutionary, that it lacks legitimacy in the higher sense, and that its legitimacy is only a surrogate for genuine, organic, and historical legitimacy. This is why the Prussian centralism of Frederick II became a revolutionary state for the romantics. In consequence, its order was not genuine. It was only a stopgap against chaos that was achieved by means of an artificial mechanism, like the state of Napoleon. Such a system of argument, therefore, is "a stick with two ends." Depending upon the end one takes hold of, it can be wielded in different directions. Adam Müller, for example, thinks that the alternative pair hammer:anvil is grounded in natural-positive law. What prevents him from setting up the following sequence?

| hammer | anvil | positive | negative |
| above | below | Christian | pagan |

It is not the substantive content of his inferences and arguments, but rather an affirmation or denial that is decided upon independently of this consideration. This affirmation or denial is the motor of a pseudoargument whose empty formulas can be adapted to any state of affairs. The assent of the romantic occasionalist weaves a web for itself that is not touched by the real external world, and thus it is not refuted either. This distinctive productivity needs to be considered in more detail.

The subject who is limited to its own experience and who, in spite of this, wants to develop a productivity because it prefers not to give up the pretension of meaning something as a subject attempts to shape its experience in an artistic fashion. This is the psychic fact that is the basis of an interest that is only aesthetic. The genial subject, who produces a work of art, is identified with God, who creates the world. The occasionalistic structure of the romantic persists, however, even in the face of this departure from the ethic of historical occasionalism. This holds true even though all the tumultuous expressions of the romantic — in terms of which many proposed to explain its nature — arose from this departure. As a Cartesian philosopher who was also influenced by the aftereffects of Scholasticism, Malebranche had brought into play intellectual elements that were too powerful to make it possible for him to ground an ethic on a mere emotive state. He does not renounce clear, rational knowledge, and he even sees the explanation of all immorality as lying in an error, which again rests on a premature judgment. We are carried away by our sensual appetites and our imagination, with the result that we want to make judgments all too impetuously. Psychologically, it is correct that a somewhat questionable specialized knowledge comes to light in his detailed account of sources of error, especially errors that have their origin in the imagination — a point that was already noticed by his contemporaries. Nevertheless, it remains decisive that in Malebranche, God, and indeed the God of traditional Christian metaphysics, is the absolute factor of his system, and Malebranche as a man stands entirely within the tradition of his age, which had still not broken up. On the other hand, the romantic with his subjectified occasionalism can make a judgment only under the most extreme pressure. Not only does he swiftly define and combine all sciences and arts, all peoples and nations, the state, the Church, and world history; and not only is he able to comprehend the essence or the "totality" of statecraft, politics, and agronomy — so that Tieck finally burst out in complaint against all the journals in which each month one finds out what the author has just learned, and in which ignorance and intellectual anarchy, twisting and distorting, discover a new philosophy every day (he names Adam Müller as an example and claims that he does not exempt even the *Athenaeum*). On the contrary, a romantic must regard it as a vital necessity, postulated on existential grounds, that one abandon oneself to the sublime play of one's imagination. In that case, one also arrives at results — which are, of course, always provisional — at pithy and striking formulations, at "antithetical" constructs and thunderous fragments that even make use of the forms of the most abstract mathematics. None of this can be linked either to a science or to ethics. The only productivity that the subject can develop in this situation is of an aesthetic sort.

In the work of art, the ordinary reality of causal relations is superseded. Without venturing into the mechanism of causality, the artist can set a creative energy in motion. The art that is the highest in the romantic sense, and in which a distinctively romantic productivity can be discerned, is the musical lyric and a kind of lyrical music. This is the source of the romantic error of regarding all music as peculiarly romantic. The great music of the sixteenth, seventeenth, and eighteenth centuries with its determinate forms of art and style is actually anything but romantic. But tones, intervals, chords, dissonances, and musical lines can be especially easily used as starting points for romantic emotions and maundering moods. Here experience can shift into associations without any further object; it can blend with other experiences in harmonies and dissonances; and it can clothe itself in song, as in the music of the lyrical poem. The mathematical formula that governs the cosmos serves as a hieroglyph for a chaos of moods. If the essence of the world is number or a geometrical figure, then music — whose essence is also number — is the essence of the world. And just as every point in the world can become the beginning point for the romantic novel and can serve as the occasion for the romantic "play of the world," so the musical line or the chord is a vessel for the most diverse contents of experience. An unbounded world of associations and intimations can be related to every melody, every chord, indeed to a single keynote. There are no limits to the possibility of interpretation. The same melody can be a frivolous love song today and a gripping song of repentance some years hence. The song that evokes secret reminiscences from a person's youth can become a banal popular song. What a boundless region for the game of associations abandoned to its own devices! The incident related by Anton Reiser has rightly been alluded to as germane to the knowledge of the romantic. As a young man, he hears in church a song that begins with the words "Hylo, lovely sun," and he is gripped by this mystical and Oriental sound. To his disappointment, he learns that the song really begins with the words "Hide, O lovely sun (the joy of your rays in the deep gossamer"). It would have been romantic to conserve for oneself a precious word as a reservoir for enormous impressionistic possibilities. To invent such a word as a receptacle of romantic affect would have been romantic productivity. The world of emotional states can be invoked by means of a sound or a musical arabesque, such as a romantic vision of the totality of the cosmos invoked by means of a mathematical figure. And just as a process of rationalization does not lie in such a figure, so the emotional state is not formed in the romantic-musical composition. It is rather that the objective of romanticism is fulfilled: A paraphrase that has no bounds, does not nullify subjective freedom, and preserves an abundance of associative possibilities is found for a content without conceptual limits. To this end, art becomes musical. A musical poetry arises, a musical form of painting and a painterly music, a general blending. It is always clearly oriented, however, to a special form of disintegrated music, and its realization, the total work of art — in other words, the hybrid work of art — was a piece of music.

The cases in which the artistic energy of a romantic succeeds in attaining a musical or a lyrical form are aesthetically interesting. In this context, we are concerned only with the distinctive quality of the productivity of political romantics such as Schlegel and Müller. Their character also lay in the echo of an activity that was not their own, and they too sought to acquire their productivity in this way. Lacking all social and intellectual stability, they succumbed to every powerful complex in their vicinity that made a claim to be taken as true reality. Thus lacking all moral scruples and any sense of responsibility other than that of a zealous and servile functionary, they could allow themselves to be used by any political system, a point that can be confirmed by the administrative activity of Adam Müller. Insofar as they developed a productivity that extends beyond this, a complication appeared that has led to many errors. In the real sense, they were not capable of shaping something in an artistic fashion. This is because they were not able to shape, either poetically or musically, the affect with which they reacted to their momentary intellectual and social surroundings. As occasionalists, they accompanied what took place around them with praise and blame, approbation and disgust. They characterized and criticized. As romantics, however, they attempted to achieve the productivity of the genial subject in precisely this fashion. The great occasionalists Geulincx and Malebranche proved to be true philosophers in their private lives as well. Here too they exhibit a stability that is a reflex of the stability of their "true cause" — that is, their concept of God. As a result, it is only with apologies and protests against misunderstandings that they can be compared with Schlegel and Müller. Their wisdom *ubi nihil vales, ibi nihil velis* [when you are worth nothing, you will nothing] could be the motto for a satire on Friedrich Schlegel and Adam Müller. These romantics, on the other hand, attempted to form their accompanying affect with intellectualized material and to preserve it with philosophical, literary, historical, and legal arguments. A new hybrid romantic artifact, composed of aesthetic, philosophical, and scientific elements, is the result. Having surrendered to the impression of the most immediate reality, they provide an intellectualistic underpinning for their feeling. They clothe affect with philosophical and scientific raiments and words rich in associations, collecting the material for this from the literature of the entire world, from all peoples, ages, and cultures. In consequence, the momentary impression of an enormous richness results. Entire worlds seem to be conquered.

In fact, they provided a stimulus for great poets and scholars, and in this way they evoked a heightened productivity. For the romantics themselves, however, this was only the general mobilization of all values, the great liquidation in the service of an accompaniment with which they followed an activity that was not their own in order to participate in it through criticism and characterizations of praise or blame. Words and impressions such as *transcendental, totality, culture, life, tradition, duration, nobility, state,* and *Church* are underpinned with an argument that is itself constituted on the basis of configurations of affect. The totality is a rational resonance in which words and arguments are fused into a lyrical political philosophy, a poetic science of finance, and a musical agronomy — everything determined by the aim, not of articulating the great impression that moves the romantic, but of paraphrasing it in an expression that makes a correspondingly great impression. The "antithetical," the antinomic, and the dialectical are conflicting emotional states. A strange sound is blended from the echo of contentious realities. The antithetical quality of speculation in the philosophy of nature and the psychology of mysticism also rest on emotive oppositions of pleasure and aversion, love and hate, joy and pain. Thus for the romantic, here there is a storehouse of idioms that are rich in moods and associations. But he uses them as a creative subject for his web that is half aesthetic and half scientific, a web that can then be a starting point for serious suggestions. That is because, in the romantic, it is not concepts of objects but expressions of moods, associations, colors, and sounds that are combined in an admixture.

In consequence, every astonishing piece of wisdom imaginable can be heard from romantic fragments and intimations, just as everything can be read out of the oracle of every horoscope. Or, to employ a simile from Malebranche, just as children hear everything that is supposed to have been said in the ringing of bells, whereas the bells have said nothing, but have only chimed.

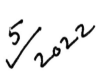

3

Political Romanticism

Survey of the development of theories of the state since 1796

The year 1796 is especially well suited for a survey of the arguments that were advanced against the French Revolution of 1789. That is because in this year the decisive conservative ideas were already completely set out. Burke's *Reflections on the Revolution in France* (1790) had also circulated outside England. Between 1790 and 1793, the Hanoverian Rehberg had published criticisms of the French Revolution in the *Jenaische Allgemeine Literaturzeitung* that were entirely in the spirit of the English Whig. In 1793, Gentz published his German translation of Burke's *Reflections*. In 1796, Bonald's *Théorie du pouvoir* was published (the manuscript had already been completed by 1794, and upon publication it was immediately confiscated by the Directorate). Finally, in the same year of 1796, de Maistre's *Considérations sur la France* also appeared, at first in Neuchâtel. In all these writings, what interests us is not the routine polemics, the case against the abomination of mob rule and Jacobin slogans, but rather the counterrevolutionary argument in principle. This is invariably the rejection of the idea that law and the state could result from the methodical activity of individual human beings. All important state institutions, and especially the constitutions that were altered so frequently during the French Revolution, are said to result automatically and in the course of time from prevailing circumstances and the nature of things. These institutions are the rational expression of such circumstances, not their creator.

Therefore, it would be absurd to propose to force things to conform to an abstract scheme. The nation and society are not overnight products of doctrinaire "fabrication." On the contrary, they are formed over long periods of time, in such a way that the individual persons involved could not survey them or even make an estimate of them. On this point, Burke — in general phrases that are often powerfully rhetorical and emotional — stresses the growth of the national community that spans generations. De Maistre still sees the individual entirely from the perspective of the theological ideas of the classical age: in his insignificance in the presence of the transcendent providential power that governs us and in whose hands the active heroes of the Revolution appear to de Maistre as automatons. Finally, as early as 1797, Bonald, a great systematic thinker, explains what is at stake with splendid precision: the opposition between liberal individualism and social solidarity. According to Bonald, the bearer of historical activity is not the individual person or the mass of individuals. It is instead society, which lives in history and constitutes itself according to definite laws, and which really constitutes the individual person as such. All three — in a vehement rejection of the metaphysicians and the philosophers, Rousseau in particular — agree that the activity of the individual, based on rationalistic maxims, can create nothing. It can only delay, destroy, and abrogate the natural course of things; but it cannot produce anything of permanence.

In Germany, there was still a belief in the Revolution. In 1793, Fichte energetically took on Rehberg's critique and the "empiricists" in his *Beiträge zur Berichtigung der Urteile des Publikums über die französische Revolution* [Contributions to the rectification of public opinion concerning the French Revolution], and he was enthusiastically resolved to dress the world in the "uniform of reason." In 1796, the eighteenth-century conception of rationalistic natural right that emanates from the individual was still completely dominant in Germany. Rousseau was celebrated by Kant as the Newton of morality, and the young Hegel mentioned him together with Socrates and Christ. In this year of 1796, Fichte published the first part of the *Grundlage des Naturrechts* [Foundation of natural right], Feuerbach published a *Kritik des natürlichen Rechts* [Critique of natural right], Friedrich Schlegel a *Versuch über den Begriff des Republikanismus* [Essay on the concept of republicanism], and Schelling wrote a *Neue Deduktion des Naturrechts* [New deduction of natural right]. In these writings, right and the state are throughout explained entirely in the sense of the eighteenth century, in terms of the coexistence of human beings: on the basis of the insight into the necessity of the self-limitation that results when free and independent beings want to live together. Right rests on a purely rational and logical consistency. It is so thoroughly a matter of the rationally calculating intellect that, to employ Kant's language, even a band of devils could found a state, provided that they have only the necessary intelligence. In short, right and the state are things to be deliberately fabricated. When Fichte, in opposition to his writing of 1793 on the Revolution, now acknowledges the lawful community as such, claiming that all right and property proceed from the state and that the individual possesses nothing prior to the political contract, he also does nothing more than reiterate *The Social Contract* of Rousseau. Individuals still constitute the state, which confronts them as an independent unity — as a *moi*, as Rousseau expresses it — only after this constitution. Thus Fichte's activism, which proposes to change the world rationally and according to "absolute causality" — a psychic disposition that might have suited a good Jacobin — also persists in 1796. Subsequently as well, Fichte — in all of his many contradictions: socialism and individualism, cosmopolitanism and nationalism — always held fast to the natural right conception of the establishment of the state by means of a contract.

In the years that followed, a current of new life seemed to flow through Germany. At Easter of 1797, Hölderlin's *Hyperion* appeared. In 1798, the *Preussische Jahrbücher* published the fragments "Glauben und Liebe" [Faith and love] by Novalis, and in 1799 his essay "Die Christenheit oder Europa" [Christianity or Europe] appeared. In the same year, Fichte noted, "Strictly speaking, philosophizing is not living, and life, strictly speaking, is not philosophizing." Also in the writings of the young Hegel from this period, in the work "The Spirit of Christianity and Its Fate," a "spirit of beauty" and love suddenly appears exalted above all obligation and all morality, a spirit that prevails over the "righteousness of the all-too-conscientious," the inhumanity of the Jewish belief in God, and everything that is "mechanical." In the fragments of Schleiermacher and Friedrich Schlegel and in the *Athenaeum*, the "legalistic" ethic of Kant and the degradation of the state to a necessary evil and a mere piece of machinery are contemptuously thrust aside. This was still not a new political philosophy, however, even though Novalis had spoken of the state as a "beautiful individual" and had called it, in connection with mystical and theosophic ideas, a macroanthropos. On the whole, the new enthusiasm was in favor of the Revolution, which was celebrated as a colossal event. Even Novalis believed he could best praise Burke by saying that he wrote a revolutionary book against the Revolution. The new sense of life was expressed in poems, novels, and fragments.

It was only later that the new political philosophy was advanced, and indeed by Schelling. It was not worked out in detail, but was rather suggested in the way of a fugitive sketch at the conclusion of philosophical systems. Even in his *System des transzendentalen Idealismus* [System of transcendental Idealism] of 1800, the entire doctrine of right had appeared to Schelling no differently from how it had appeared to Fichte and the eighteenth century: as a mechanism in which free beings are conceived in interaction. The state is designated as an organism in the specific sense only under the influence of Hegel and after the dissociation from Fichte. This was in Schelling's *Vorlesungen über die Methode des akademischen Studiums* [Lectures on the method of academic study], which appeared in 1803. Here the reproach of mechanism is raised only against the state of "civil law." It is not raised against the true state, which transforms everything that is private into public law: the objective organism of freedom and the "natural aspect of the Church." Kantian natural right theoreticians and Fichte too are charged with wanting to "make up" a state, and with creating nothing but an infinite mechanism. But for all that, this state is still capable of improvement. It is supposed to be a work of art created on the basis of "ideas." This last residue of a "task" disappears in the Würzburg lectures of 1804, *System der gesamten Philosophie* [System of philosophy as a whole]. Here Schelling achieved the serene and tranquil grandeur of Spinoza. The state *is* in the idea. It is something that exists, not something moral or something that has to be brought about. It is instead a work of art in which science, religion, and art interpenetrate one another to form a homogeneous and spiritual organism. It is a spiritual sphere with the three powers just named as its attributes. In it, philosophy and the Church are objectified in a vital, rhythmic, and harmonic beauty — that is, in an artistically correct fashion.

This idea of the state — as noted, only fleetingly suggested at the conclusion of Schelling's systems — had one defect in the eyes of romanticism: it was "loveless wisdom" (Schleiermacher). In the same year of 1804, Friedrich Schlegel began his Paris-Cologne lectures in which he set out what was essential to romanticism: the feelings of love and fidelity. They were alleged to be the most stable pillars of civil life. A further explanation of this view of the state is not provided. The lectures are concerned with the construction of a state organized into four estates (two lower estates, the peasants and the bourgeoisie; and two higher estates, the nobility and the clergy). This construction conforms to similar theories that were articulated by Schelling, Hegel, and J. J. Wagner and advocate an estatist monarchy. Making use of traditionalistic theories — as articulated in the writings of Bonald that had already appeared by that time — Schlegel postulated the feudal hereditary state. In addition, these lectures include ideas from Fichte, such as the socialist demand for superior state property and the strictest control of all economic life and trade. In short, we find here a reiteration of views that were already familiar. Only the combination of feudal and socialist ideas is of interest, and only the emphasis on the emotive basis of the state is characteristic. The state composed by Adam Müller in the lectures *Ueber das Ganze der Staatskunst* (1808–1809) [On statecraft as a whole] is distinguished by this same nuance of the emotive. Here Müller, who was probably initiated into the philosophy of nature by Schelver, contrasts the state as "idea" with the lifeless, mechanical "concept" of the state, adopting Schelling's expressions rather literally. The state is supposed to be the "totality of all human affairs," the embodiment of psychic and intellectual life; and all oppositions — especially the opposition of the estates (nobility, clergy, and bourgeoisie) necessary for the articulation of the organism, but also the opposition of person and thing — are combined in a grand, vital, and organic unity. Insofar as the nature of this state is life, diversity, and movement, it belongs to Schelling's philosophy of nature. But — and this is Müller's distinctively romantic quality — it is not construed as in Schelling. This state is the object of the most fervent love. It can demand everything from us. Moreover, we are obliged to give everything to it with love, with "heart, sympathy, and feeling." Just as in Friedrich Schlegel, where the feelings of love and fidelity are to breathe life into a state compounded of traditionalistic and Fichtean elements, so here as well Schelling's idea of the "organism" already qualifies as life, but not as life filled with feeling.

The practical consequence of these theories is the advocacy of a monarchy that is half feudal and half estatist. Whereas the Revolution is celebrated up to 1799 (in the *Athenaeum*, Schlegel had still claimed that the revolutionary desire of realizing the kingdom of God was the elastic point for progressive culture and the beginning of modern history), in 1799, the year in which Schlegel became acquainted with Burke, the conservative turn begins. At that point, a philosophy that represents itself as a spiritual revolution — for Schlegel it is Fichte, for Müller, Schelling — is used in order to arrive at a theoretical foundation for feudal and conservative results. And in the year 1810 — that is, the year in which Müller became acquainted with Bonald's writings — a sudden turn again takes place. Now the hitherto prevailing philosophy of nature is repudiated as "atheism" and a "fraud." Instead of the ideas of dynamic life, Bonald's traditionalistic argument is taken over, and subsequently it is combined with the arguments of Haller and de Maistre. At this juncture, Burke becomes less significant, although as a conservative political figure, he is, of course, still mentioned respectfully. His restless pathos, however, which earlier had such a decisive influence, no longer conforms to the mood of the restoration, and his views on parliament and constitution are disagreeable to monarchist theory. Bonald and de Maistre had a less enthusiastic relationship to emotionality. Bonald's explanations are quite sober. Given the necessary political stability of the state, love and fidelity follow automatically. And in the classical description of a counterrevolution given in the ninth chapter of de Maistre's *Considérations,* we discover the sovereign skepticism with which he conceived the feelings of the people. Thus "movement" disappears, and in its place *fixité* appears. During the restoration, even Metternich's centralized police state becomes organic, durable, supportive, stable, peaceful, and legitimate to the romantics. Now *originality* is a suspicious predicate, and no one has talked about irony for a long time.

The difference between the romantic conception of the state and the counterrevolutionary and legitimist conception

This survey of the development of political ideas among the romantics shows that the romantic sense of the world and life can be combined with the most diverse political circumstances and with antithetical philosophical theories. As long as the Revolution is present, political romanticism is revolutionary. With the termination of the Revolution, it becomes conservative, and in a markedly reactionary restoration it also knows how to extract the romantic aspect from such circumstances. After 1830, romanticism becomes revolutionary again, and even the aging Bettina discovered extremely revolutionary accents in her book on the king (1843) and in the *Gespräche mit Dämonen* (1851) [Conversations with demons]. This variability of political content is not accidental. On the contrary, it is a consequence of the occasionalist attitude, and it is deeply rooted in the nature of the romantic, the essence of which is passivity.

Of course, it seems obvious that the rejection of conscious "fabrication" common to all counterrevolutionary theories or the quietism of a theory of legitimacy should be identified with the political passivity of the romantics. All the founders of the counterrevolutionary theory, however — Burke, de Maistre, and Bonald — were active politicians, each with his own responsibility. For years, they maintained a tenacious and energetic opposition against their governments. They were always filled with the sense that they were not elevated above the political struggle, but were instead obligated to decide in favor of what they regarded as right. Even traditionalism in its most rigorously consistent rejection of all individual reason is not necessarily passive. The idea of humanity implicit in traditionalism can also demonstrate its revolutionary force here. The *Paroles d'un croyant* by such a resolute traditionalist as Lamennais provides a colossal example of this force. But as his contemporaries already perceived and as a theological opponent of traditionalism, J. Lupus, correctly stresses, the path from Malebranche leads directly to the unconditional passivism that destroys all activity.[1] Thus the subjectified occasionalism of the romantic also accompanies what encounters it, and it should not be difficult to differentiate its organic passivity from the restraints of an active statesman that result from political experience and objectives. The criterion is whether the ability to make a decision between right and wrong is present. This ability is the principle of every political energy: the revolutionary, which appeals to natural right or human rights, as well as the conservative, which appeals to historical right. The legitimist philosophy also recognizes the distinction between right and wrong. It only juxtaposes rights that are historically well earned to the natural right distinction between right and mere de facto power. When God appears as the ultimate principle of political life in legitimist theories of political philosophy, he has this status as the highest sovereign and lawgiver, as the ultimate point of legitimation, and thus in a normative — and thereby antiromantic — category. As de Maistre expresses himself, history is only God's prime minister in the department of this world. In the case of Burke as well, the pathos that dominated him in the face of the Revolution is never the aesthetic feeling of the romantics, who saw the Revolution as a grandiose drama or an event of nature. For Burke, the Revolution is a shocking violation of divine and human right. We need only compare the effeminate raptures that those two bourgeois literati Schlegel and Müller summoned up on behalf of the aristocracy with Burke's obstinate defense of the emigrants in order to see the great difference between them.

In the consciousness of right of the Revolution — which is based on natural right doctrines — these counterrevolutionaries see nothing but a judgment confused by human passions and metaphysical abstractions. They regard a natural right as something that is self-evident, however, and they do not exhibit the fundamental inability to comprehend it, of which Adam Müller boasts in his lectures of 1808–1809. In the romantic, the "organic" conception of the state rests on this inability to make a normative evaluation. This conception repudiates the "juridical" as narrow and mechanical, and it searches for the state that is above right and wrong: that is, a point of reference for feelings, which at the same time is a projection of the romantic subject into the domain of the political. The root of romantic sublimity is the inability to decide, the "higher third" factor they are always talking about, which is not a higher factor but a different third factor: in other words, it is always a way out of the either-or. Because they leave the decision open — because they construe the *occasio* "antithetically," so that it can be the elastic point for the leap to the "higher third" factor — there has been talk of their "dualism," and reminders of gnostic and Neoplatonic theories have been found, where what was at stake was only the lack of an object that is characteristic of an occasionalism.

Even the essay on "the signature of the age" that Friedrich Schlegel published in *Concordia* (1820–1823) — an essay that is full of the mood of the restoration — is a convincing proof and, for several reasons, a useful illustration of the difference between political romanticism and the counterrevolutionary theory of the state. On all essential points, Schlegel is in agreement with Müller's views. He uses many of Müller's favorite turns of phrase ("legal machinery," "locale," the "English malady," and so on), and like Müller he especially repudiates all "ultras." His exposition is written in a composed frame of mind. It is a cohesive account that lends itself to discussion. The loud ejaculations of early romanticism are rejected. It turns out that there are even characterizations of this stage that must be called admirable: "superficial-dynamic-permutational thought," an "intellectual game of dice," "scientific fantasizing," the "Babylonian linguistic confusion of an immature philosophy." In the final analysis, untruthfulness and verbosity. It is true that the essay seems to be almost completely free of impulses that, at first sight, would be called romantic. Only in one passage does a high-romantic passage resound. If the true state did not protect us from the despotic state, "then every reasonable person would surely prefer the state of nature, not as poets describe it or as theoreticians imagine it, but rather as we become acquainted with it through history: namely (and here there are resonances of Herder's *Hebräische Poesie* [Hebraic poetry]), the free life of nomads and armed tribes of herdsmen under the leadership of family chieftains and tribal princes, such as the times of Abraham make known to us, and in part is still found in Arabia. Then one would gladly give up the wretched tinsel of our culture for the abundance of this sense of nature." In addition, there is a superficial manifestation of the good influence of Catholicism, in the face of which the melancholy cloud of early romanticism evaporated. One also notices that romanticism had reservations about the restoration, and that it anticipated another age.

And yet in its core, the essay is thoroughly romantic. It manifests its signature especially clearly in the endeavor to provide a forceful definition of how it differs from other political views of the restoration period, especially the views of the French royalists. These distinctions and certain psychologically acute characterizations of men of Schlegel's time — Gentz, for example — constitute the significance of the essay. Otherwise its content is unoriginal to the point of banality. What does the distinctive quality of Schlegel's world view consist in, compared to that of Bonald, for example, who is also supposed to be a "political romantic"? It lies in the romantic. Bonald is a theoretician. He is fond of abstract formulas. He undertakes discussions of fundamental principles, and in morality and politics he wants to arrive at the compelling certainty of the laws of mathematics and natural science. In all this, he was a person who stood for his convictions in political reality, and he had an extremely unromantic aversion to fantasies, reveries, and lyric poems. For this reason, he was active during the restoration in France as the leader of the "ultras," who combated the quasi-liberal and constitutional policy of the government with all political means. He fought for the "natural system of societies" against the "political system of the cabinet."[2] Regardless of how this standpoint may be judged politically, regardless of whether it is regarded as justified or narrow minded, a man who took his political convictions seriously had to come to this kind of political activity.

The romantic Schlegel is altogether different. In spite of some disagreements over the historical assessment of individual persons and events, his views and ideals correspond to those of Bonald's. Like Bonald, he demands an estatist monarchy with a Christian-Catholic foundation. He is shocked, however, by the mere thought that his ideals might be defended in political practice. He has political ideals. But he implores the reader not to believe that the author has the presumption of making even the most trifling changes in existing conditions. So what does he really want? He wants to "follow" the development "as a sympathetic fellow traveler." He is "concerned only with a purely intellectual discussion and elucidation of the age." He does not want to be one of the "self-appointed world reformers," regardless of whether their intentions are good or bad. The "purely intellectual discussion and elucidation of the age," however, does not rule out personal evaluations on the part of the author. It does not mean that the author only wants to explain matters scientifically. On the contrary, the essay is supposed to prove that the times are evil and governed by an evil principle. The wickedness is supposed to consist precisely in wanting to do something politically. For him, political passion and political polemics are unchristian. The "ultra spirit," like every partisan spirit, is evil. A Christian should not belong to any party, and to form even a Catholic party would be a "wanton desecration" of Catholicism. Bonald despised capricious and unhistorical experimentation in political matters. But he took it as self-evident that one would also really have to combat what he regarded as an unhistorical politics. The romantic uses the word *historical* as a cover for his passivity, just as he uses Christianity. With the corporative-estatist ideals that he advocates, the romantic cannot be a supporter of Metternich's centralized state. He also points this out repeatedly. And yet the entire essay served this system. It has the concrete political purpose of opposing the general demand for representative constitutions — a demand based on the constitutional promise of Article 13 of the Acts of the Federal Parliament — and advocating estatist-corporative constitutions. Like Müller's statements along the same lines, its polemic against the "ultras" conformed to Metternich's intention, who on April 9, 1819, had written to Gentz as follows: "My daily struggle is against ultras of every sort." Although Görres is a writer who can be "counted among the defenders of Christian theories of the state in general," he is reproached for continuing to vacillate between corporative principles and "the usual representative illusion." As regards specifics, there is "much that is incorrect" in his writing, and he is a German "doctrinaire." The French constitutional center party under Royer-Collard was also characterized as "doctrinaire." That was sufficient to dispose of Görres, for here again we have a party, even if it is a moderate one. Royalists, Catholics, and legitimists have an ultra party. The liberals and the progressives are a negative party. Nationalism is a partisan evil. Moderates stand in the middle and are also merely a party. But we cannot be indifferent either. That is explicitly emphasized; for it would be wicked, Schlegel claims, to be indifferent to the good principle. In this case, what should we do? We should agree to what the government does. This is what our activity amounts to: assent.

The government is the higher, inclusive third factor, elevated above the oppositions of the parties. It should pay heed to the parties of neither the right nor the left. Above all, it should not choose to be a moderate center, because in this position it would be only a passive center. Schlegel also regards it, however, as inadmissible to speak of an active center. "The solution to the big problem does not lie at the ends and the extremes and not in the middle, but rather only and exclusively in the depths and the heights." In the face of the power of the government, the oppositions between parties are supposed "to disappear into nothingness like a phantom." Here even Napoleon appeals to him, because Napoleon's government had the power to crush the parties. There is no right of resistance against the ruling authorities. Bonald approves of the refusal of the old Parisian parliament to put a law on the books that contradicted the "nature of societal relations." He took pleasure in the *nec possumus, nec debemus* [we neither can do it, nor are obliged to do it] that was opposed to the king.[3] On the whole, he has sympathy for republican independence, and he wants it to become an element of the French monarchy.[4] In his essay, Schlegel also speaks of the right of resistance, but of course very cautiously and in passing. And yet he must concede the possibility of a justified resistance, for as a Catholic he cannot doubt that one must obey God more than man. It is only the Church, however, that should decide whether such a case obtains. Indeed, this circumstance is the essential condition for the necessity of a church (p. 390). For a moment, it seems as if an even higher "order," the Church, were introduced here. And in fact, this passage proves that here the romantic stood in the field of force of another political reality, the Church. Happily, Schlegel was not forced to a practical decision, for matters did not come to a conflict between Austria and the Church. But he did not make a theoretical decision either. In another passage (p. 189), he rejects as "unhistorical" de Maistre's resolute advocacy of the Church's right of control. In relation to secular states, the Church is not supposed to have any legal control and any position as arbitrator. That was justified until the sixteenth century. It is no longer feasible, however, for our times, nor can it return. In the end, therefore, nothing is changed. The paramount activity of the government is not endangered by the opposition between Church and state. And yet this very government, the only thing that is permitted to act, experiences the same fate as the God of the occasionalist system. It is not supposed to do anything that is "arbitrary," "mechanical," and "absolute." Actually, it should simply abandon itself to historical development. In the occasionalist system, what was called the general order in which God's activity disappeared is here sometimes called historical development, and sometimes organic development. Practically, the same point *f₁: This avoids responsibility for social life. Society is deified. In contrast, Rousseau forces humanity to take responsibility for the matrix we created.*

f₂: In terms of Feuerbach, God talk is man talk. So, the irony is their is never an escape from human action; just a veil over it viz "God talk"

that holds for the individual also holds for the political activity of the government: It should not "want to bring something about," but should only pulsate in the rhythm of the nomological event. History, development, and, ultimately, Divine Providence are the final authorities, to which even the government is obliged to relinquish all real activity.

Thus all activity is shifted from one place to another: from the individual to the government, and from the government to God. And in God, activity is providence and nomological necessity. The individual factors occasionally change their names. The government can also be called the state — as in Müller's *Elemente der Staatskunst*. Schlegel inserts history between the government and God. The idea of the "organism" can also be placed in the service of occasionalist evasion and can ground an "organic development" as the only final authority that is operative. In short, the simple sequence of the occasionalist system is confused in romanticism by the blending of the single factors with romanticized concepts of the philosophy of the time. Nevertheless, romanticism remains clearly recognizable. Regardless of whether the final and inclusive member of the sequence is called God or the state, the ego or history, the idea or organic development, the result is invariably that all activity of the individual person consists in the fact that he is a "sympathetic fellow traveler." The result is the same in political life: one should not interfere with what the competent authorities do. Even when Müller and Schlegel call the age evil and juxtapose the good principle to an evil one, this is not to be understood as a moral decision. They do not propose to take sides, which everyone has to do who speaks of good and evil in the moral sense and distinguishes right from wrong. Thus Burke, de Maistre, and Bonald took sides against the French Revolution because they thought it was wrong, and from the beginning Gentz declared that the question of the legitimacy of the Revolution was "the first and the last."[5] Adam Müller, on the other hand, finds no immediate moral pathos in the face of the Revolution. Nothing is more characteristic for political romanticism than its judgment on the French Revolution, in which it remained steadfast. "The history of the French Revolution is a proof, pursued throughout thirty years,

f₃: Here Schmitt in his way is addressing your question of responsibility.

of the truth that, independently and without religion, man cannot break any of the chains that oppress him without sinking into a more abject slavery. Just how little is achieved in the way of the mere breaking of the chains, regardless of how intrinsically laudable the emotion necessary for that may be, I have already shown in 1810 in my lectures on Frederick the Great and the Prussian monarchy." Thus the question of the justification of the Revolution is settled with an ironically spiteful remark. Here we should note that in these lectures of 1810 (p. 305) Müller had really characterized the Revolution as a manifestation of oppressed and fettered life. Now, however, he rejects it and openly declares that he is not interested in whether it was justified. So how did he arrive at his rejection? In the same way he arrives at affirmations. They are accompanying emotional states with which he sympathetically follows historical development, because he is really interested only in feeling and poetry.

The state and the king as occasional objects of romantic interest

Concretely expressed, this means the following: romantically, revolution and restoration can be taken in the same way. In other words, they can be made into the occasion for the romantic interest in the same way. It is false and misleading to characterize the ideas — or even the emotive and emotional world — of legitimism as "political romanticism" in the specific sense. The romantic subject can regard distinctly heterogeneous and antithetical processes and configurations as the beginning of the romantic novel. Without changing its nature and its structure, which invariably remain occasionalist, romantic productivity can be linked to any other object of historical-political reality besides just the legitimate sovereign. When Novalis celebrates the king and the charming queen in poetry, and when Adam Müller does the same for feudal agrarian conditions, this is of no importance for either a monarchist, a feudal, an estatist, or even a legitimist theory of the state. Here the king is no less occasional than a "colossal" revolutionary hero, a bandit, or a courtesan is for other romantics. From the standpoint of the romantic interest, that is really self-evident. For if emotion, poetry, and charm are the decisive qualities, then it can easily happen that many eminently legitimist phenomena appear less interesting and less "romantic" than the pretty young girls dancing around a freedom tree. Unfortunately, there is no necessary connection between poetic beauty and legitimacy, and the taste of the age changes quickly. The geniuses of the Young Germany movement of the following generation already romanticized Napoleon and proved that in revolution one can see (like the romantics of 1799 already did) an impressive drama of grandiose movement that is just as romantic as that mellow image of traditional conditions that appear romantically in the impressive illustration of the gray old man, melting into the immemorial past. The two do not contradict each other. That is because both can be a theme for romanticizing. Legitimacy, however, is an absolutely unromantic category. The question of whether the drama that has Danton as its main character is more romantic than another drama whose hero is perhaps Otto the Idle cannot be decided according to the perspectives of legitimacy. It is only poeticization that breathes romantic life into the object, even where we are concerned with a figure of historical reality. Before being poeticized, it was dead and romantically inconsequential, regardless of what sort of political significance it might have.

The romantic incapacity for ethical and legal valuation

Any relationship to a legal or moral judgment would be incongruous here, and every norm would seem to be an antiromantic tyranny. A legal or a moral decision would be senseless and it would inevitably destroy romanticism. This is why the romantic is not in a position to deliberately take sides and make a decision. On romantic grounds, he cannot even decisively reject the theory of the state that proceeds from the view that man is "evil by nature." Even if many romantics find this theory uncongenial, there is still the possibility of romanticizing this wicked person, the "beast," as long as he only remains sufficiently remote. From the standpoint of romanticism, what is at stake is something higher than a decision. The self-consciousness of early romanticism — which allowed itself to be carried along by the energy of the other irrational movements of its time and also played the absolute ego and the creator of the universe — experienced this as superiority. But when, in spite of these considerations, certain typical romantics such as Friedrich Schlegel and Adam Müller occupied themselves both theoretically and practically with political problems posed by the times, it turned out that they repeated Burke, Bonald, de Maistre, and Haller. In other words, it turned out that there is no political productivity in the romantic. Now romantics preach complete passivity. They employ mystical, theological, and traditionalistic ideas such as resignation, humility, and permanence in order to make Metternich's police into a worthy object of affectionate attachment and to fuse the superior authorities with the higher third factor.

Romanticized ideas in political philosophy

This, therefore, is the core of all political romanticism: The state is a work of art. The state of historical-political reality is the occasion for the work of art produced by the creative achievement of the romantic subject. It is the occasion for poetry and the novel, or even for a mere romantic mood. When Novalis speaks of the state as a macroanthropos, this is an idea that has been expressed for centuries. Romanticism obtains only when this state-person is called a "beautiful" individual and is the object of love and similar feelings. We find an extreme but entirely consistent example of this purely aesthetic and sentimental conduct in the romantic conception of the Prussian state. Novalis and Adam Müller agree in pronouncing the Prussia of Frederick II, the bachelor and apostle of the Enlightenment, to be an empty machine and a factory. On the other hand, they regard the Prussia of the consort of the charming Queen Luise as a true kingdom and the most beautiful, poetic, and natural form of the state. Frederick II, however, can also be the point of departure for a romantic interest. In that case, the romantic picture itself changes. The dignity of the monarchy rests on a "poetry" that forces itself on the person and satisfies a higher longing of his nature. The simple consequence of this aesthetic political philosophy seems to be that the most beautiful person should govern the state: that first in beauty should be first in might (Keats). But again, that would not be romantic, for in the romantic it is not reality that matters, but rather romantic productivity, which transforms everything and makes it into the occasion for a poetry. What the king and the queen are in reality is intentionally ignored. Their function consists instead in being a point of departure for romantic feelings. The same holds for the beloved. From the standpoint of romanticism, therefore, it is simply not possible to distinguish between the king, the state, or the beloved. In the twilight of the emotions, they blend into one another. In both Novalis and Adam Müller, the state appears as the beloved, and the poeticizing of the science of finance that they bring off lies in the consideration that one should pay taxes to the state just as one gives presents to the beloved. So it is all one whether Novalis writes a poem to the Virgin Mary or Müller writes a chapter on the state. Applied to concrete historical situations, this kind of productivity results in the charming idyll of the Middle Ages that Novalis has sketched in his famous essay "Christianity or Europe." In its content, mood, and cadence, the essay is a fairy tale. It is not an intellectual achievement, but rather a beautiful poetic fantasy. It belongs with Rousseau's description of the state of nature in the *Discourse on the Origin and Foundations of Inequality*. But it is not treated as a fairy tale, and even today it is quoted with pedantic seriousness in the same breath as the utterances of responsible statesmen and philosophical thinkers and is given equal weight as proof. This fact is also the result of the romantic obliteration of all categories. It is a sign of the subromantic inability to recognize the style of an intellectual expression.

Adam Müller himself has found fine words for the sublimity of the state and the contemptuousness of the humanistic, individualistic culture of the personality in his time. But what is the "state" to which he contrasts this culture in his *Elemente der Staatskunst*? It is a projection of the romantic subject into the political, a superindividual that is supposed to have the single individual as its natural function. It claims to be the "object of infinite love," and it enters into all conceivable oppositions and polarities: man and woman, nobility and bourgeoisie, war and peace, justice and utility, city and country — in short, the romantic quest for the reality that is sought for. As a result, in 1810, it can readily be transposed into Bonald's hereditary state, and in 1819 even into Haller's state constructed entirely on the basis of civil rights. The productivity that Müller expends here should be evaluated in a purely aesthetic fashion, to the extent that it is not a thoroughly devious opportunism. For him, as for Novalis, the state was the beloved, Sophie, that can transform itself into everything and into which everything can be transformed, the object of an emotional state, and as such occasional: today Prussia and tomorrow Austria; sometimes "sovereign" and sometimes a "national energy" or the "totality of credit," a product of its own vibrations that oscillates in a "globular form," a product that it would be a desecration to approach with legal or moral concepts.

Adam Müller's productivity: his mode of argumentation: the rhetorically formed resonance of significant impressions; his antitheses: rhetorical contrasts

It does not matter that Novalis once said he was "thoroughly unjuridical." Perhaps either he or another romantic once claimed the contrary of himself as well. More important than this is the antipathy that they all have had against Kant's juridical treatment of ethics. In opposition to this, however, one could point to their fanatical interest in the Catholic church. Because of the subjective freedom of Protestantism, the Catholic church appeared to many Protestants as a vast institution for the juridification of Christianity; and when Schlegel and Müller postulated the "positivity" of Christianity, they recognized the Catholic church in exactly this form. The decision however, — the complete incompatibility of the romantic with any moral, legal, or political standard — follows only from the structure of the romantic as an occasionalist consent oriented to aesthetic productivity. Here experience is no doubt in quest of an artistic expression, but not logical-conceptual or moral-normative clarity. This is why the romantic lacks any sense of the limits of the efficacy of the state as well as the limits of the individual.

Adam Müller's amoral appreciation of everything and its opposite; his passion for mediating everywhere; his "cosmic tolerance," which so alarmed Gentz because in that case "there is no longer anything that one could love and honestly hate"; his effeminate passivity, to which he knew how to bend the aversion of Burke, de Maistre, and Bonald for artificial "fabrication"; and his emotional pantheism, which is basically always in agreement with everything and approves of everything — all this can probably be explained in an individual-psychological fashion as well, as a consequence of his feminine and vegetative nature. For romantic aestheticism, however, all these factors amounted to the appropriate psychic and physical disposition. That is because they referred the subject entirely to its own emotional states and to the aesthetic productivity that is satisfied with the elaboration of affect. Müller can do nothing but pursue an occupation with himself, regardless of whether he is engaging in astrology (or today in psychoanalysis, or at some future point perhaps in astrology again) or composing his rejection of the aestheticism of others. When he had become an unconditional and sincere Catholic, his lack of scientific and political productivity was manifested in a cheap hyperorthodoxy. In all this, there was nothing essentially individualistic. He was always ready to surrender himself. Nevertheless, he at least wanted to extract portentous words and images from the emotional state of surrender. This was his activity. For the rest, he stood with his material at the immediate disposal of every powerful suggestion. Because he was without his own center of gravity and was not constrained by matter-of-fact experience and his own responsibility, the consistency of the view that impressed him at any given time easily carried him to the extremes of its program. In Göttingen he became subject to Anglomania, in the feudal milieu of Berlin he became extremely feudal, in the clerical sphere of Vienna extremely clerical. In this regard, subjectivistic reserve is, in part, also manifested as a paradox. Even in an orthodox milieu, he tries to find a foothold for a paradoxical Fronde in the most extreme orthodoxy. Because he is not burdened by his own social substance, he automatically rises into the vicinity of the magnetic field of a socially dominant stratum. This is where he has the social reality whose resonance he can shape. It would be an error, however, to interpret his irresponsible subjectivism as aristocratic individualism, and to interpret his incapacity for a greater community transcending subjective affect as aristocratic exclusivity. Where a political or social risk is involved, he finds the political *Enragés* frankly distasteful.

He can understand everything and approve it at his pleasure. That is because everything can become material for his work of aesthetic formation. The master of the *Lehre vom Gegensatz* was incapable of seeing any polarity except that of an aesthetic contrast. Neither logical distinctions, nor moral value judgments, nor political decisions are possible for him. The most important source of political vitality, the belief in justice and an indignation over injustice, does not exist for him. What he says about Napoleon is literary demonization. The nations do not fear Napoleon, he writes in 1805, but rather the "fate that is in him." And finally, the romantic identification, which decomposes the political complex into a subjective "elongation," is not wanting either: Bonaparte's domination means only that "we learn to overcome the Bonaparte that we bear in ourselves."[6] He lacks a sense of his own right as well as any social self-esteem. On one occasion, he uses this as an effective pose in order to play the bourgeois offended by attacks on the nobility.[7] The fact that the Tyroleans — who, in spite of all guarantees, had their constitution taken from them — were done an injustice, and that he collaborated in this himself was something he simply did not notice. He had proclamations and newspaper articles to compose that had a different theme. What gives the poems of Arndt their power — political hatred and outrage over the injustice of foreign domination — is missing in every romantic utterance.

Of course the clear facts of the case are often confused because political romanticism takes over the material with which it clothes itself only in a state in which it has already been processed. Perhaps a political lyric or a song results from the immediate impression of a political fact, but not political romanticism. On the contrary, there must be on hand complete complexes of arguments, images, and pregnant — or, more accurately, suggestive — turns of phrase with which the specifically romantic productivity can develop itself in order to produce, at least superficially, a chain of conclusions and results. Arguments that have already been formulated as such can be accentuated and stressed, rhetorically embellished with trills, and "antithetically" contrasted. This is how Adam Müller handles Burke. What Gutzkow said about Chateaubriand — that he could not have given the legitimist party anything except the mellifluousness of his speech — holds true even more for Adam Müller and, where he becomes political, even for Friedrich Schlegel. The new historical sense and the awakening sense of patriotism are not to be attributed to romanticism. No more than the romantics created Catholicism were the historical sense and patriotism discovered, created, or decisively influenced by them. Whoever listens to Adam Müller speaking about Burke must, of course, think that Müller was the very first to have discovered Burke and to have introduced his work into Germany. He acts as the representative of the Burkean spirit in Germany, although compared to the excellent and important works of Brandes, Rehberg, and Gentz, his enthusiasm for Burke is substantively inconsequential. Even today, Burke is regarded in Germany as a precursor of romanticism, as if his status in romanticism were different from that of Dante, Calderón, and Goethe: a grand sonority in the hodgepodge work of art produced by romantic intellectualism, a romantic figure comparable to Beethoven in Bettina's epistolary novels, a nebulous image blending with others, "like clouds melting into one another."

When Burke discourses on duration or the national community and rises to a grandiose rhetoric, he always remains the statesman with a great responsibility: He wants to make a case to a public of normal human beings and defend it before them. When Friedrich Schlegel becomes enraptured with the French Revolution, he reproduces the impressions made on him by a varied reading and conversations with his acquaintances in Berlin and Jena. The subject matter interests him only as a "vehicle for a conversation." This is expressed in the occasional and high-romantic composite that blends three heterogeneous, but simultaneous and equally powerful impressions: the French Revolution, Fichte's *Wissenschaftslehre*, and Goethe's *Wilhelm Meister*. Schlegel had certainly not read Burke by this point. What effect did the reading of Burke have on him? August Wilhelm Schlegel had been acquainted with writings by Burke since 1791. At least he drew his brother's attention to this fact in the same year. In the meantime, Novalis had also become acquainted with Burke. In 1798, he mentions Burke in the "Pollen Fragments" (number 104), and the essay "Christianity or Europe" already exhibits Burke's influence. Friedrich Schlegel read Burke around the beginning of 1799. The effect: The idea of also writing something so "impetuous" "chokes him up."[8] Thus when Novalis says that Burke wrote a "revolutionary" book against the Revolution, this is a good characterization of the impression it made on the romantics: on Novalis, on Friedrich Schlegel, and also on Adam Müller. At that time, *revolutionary* was still synonymous with *romantic*. But the antirevolutionary could also be romantic. In other words, an incitement to aesthetic admiration and imitation was seen in both, in the French Revolution and in Burke's magnificent pathos and powerful temperament. The things Burke is concerned with, his historical sensibility, his sense of national community, his aversion to forced "fabrication" — everything that has a historical and political significance for him is transposed into another sphere and romanticized. The process of romanticizing takes place without the capacity and the possibility of objective reflection. It is the "fabulous" — at that time, one said romantic — impression of a person, a historical event, a philosophical, artistic, or literary achievement.

In consequence, Burke could also stand beside the French Revolution, Fichte, and Goethe. Adam Müller really did place him beside Goethe in this way. Napoleon and Beethoven also prove to be romantic figures. In addition, Novalis could name his friend or beloved. Schlegel and Müller also make whatever compounds and admixtures that occur to them. In their case, however, the process of romanticizing is more successful with "ideas": in other words, with material that is already at hand in intellectual formulations, which they antithetically convert into its opposite, combine with another material, effectively stylize, or romantically modify in a similar fashion. It struck Rehberg as well as Jean Paul that Adam Müller always occupied himself only with the greatest and best writers and cited only them. Müller himself seems to have found a proof of his own greatness in this consideration. When he took on Buchholz, he explicitly noted that he undertook a defense of the nobility against Buchholz only by way of an exception and because of the special circumstances of the case. In general, he would do this only if he had men such as Burke or Montesquieu as opponents. Nevertheless, these pretensions no more demonstrate a special richness in his own thinking than the constant attachment to aristocratic society in his life demonstrates his own economic wealth or an independent social position. The romantic interest in famous names is based on a different motive. A great name is a reservoir of suggestions. The works of a great man contain so many objectifications of spiritual values that "in order to be a prophet, one only needs to put his tongue or his hand in motion with a fine sense for their fingering, their tempo, their musical spirit, and the delicate effect of their inner nature."[9] Here we also find a basis for the romantic inclination for Catholicism that, thus far, has always been overlooked. In the course of a millennium of intellectual work in the Catholic church and its theology, all human problems were discussed in the highest form they can have: namely, theologically. This was a mighty arsenal of easily managed concepts and thoughtful formulas. Without venturing into the laborious and thankless work of dogmatic investigations, the romantics — just as they formerly employed the terminology of the philosophy of nature — now make use of words such as *grace, Original Sin,* and *revelation,* which serve as precious vessels into which the romantic experience overflows.

Müller, therefore, is a more pure type of the political romantic. That is because, to a higher degree than Schlegel or the other romantics, he had a specific talent that even made the technique of political romanticizing plain to him. His chief faculty is the oratorical. In his model sentences, there are examples of a *bel canto* of speech that scarcely reappear in German prose. In the long run, the cadence of his carefully prepared lectures is somewhat uniform. His imperturbable solemnity and pedantic elegance must have been indigestible for a nervous person such as Brentano. In conversation, however, when he could rely upon the thoughts of others, in a circle of acquaintances whose friendly sympathy and physical and spiritual proximity animated him, and in letters in which he knew that the recipient was prepossessed in his favor, he exhibited a fascinating wealth of words full of allusions and a sure instinct in the use of all rhetorical techniques — even an unconscious *cursus* that would have done honor to an initiate of the curial style. When we add to this his clairvoyant sense for the style of his society and an infinite capacity for assimilation, we can understand the delight so many distinguished persons have expressed. In the case of Gentz, who had a powerful rhetorical gift himself and sensed here an oratorical talent that was perhaps even superior to his own, pleasure mounts to a boundless enthusiasm. This probably explains his friendship with Müller. Here we have the source of the judgments on which he based Müller's fame among his contemporaries. He called Müller "one of the greatest minds of the age" and "the premier genius of Germany," judgments that had such a great impact as publicity that they passed into the articles published in biographical lexicons as well as into many incidental remarks: Müller, he was the man Gentz called the premier genius of Germany. If even in 1919 he can still appear as "the most mature political thinker of romanticism," then he owes that to these suggestive epigrams of his good friend Gentz. The expectations that the young Müller provoked, however, in conversations among friends such as Kurnatowski, Finkenstein, Peterson, and Gentz, who was always inclined to sincere admiration of his friends, were also immense, especially with regard to his *Lehre vom Gegensatz*. Like others, Gentz must have seen in Müller a new prophet, whom he also regarded as a powerful ally. He regarded Müller in all seriousness as the man who would overthrow Fichte, "this Baal," and indeed, by means of the *Lehre* — in contrast to Fichte's, this "great and good philosophy."

The hatred that Gentz, a cultured man of the eighteenth century, felt in the face of the raving ego-imperialism of a philosophy professor is understandable. Wilhelm von Humboldt also turned away full of disgust from this mad "chasing after ideas," and he saw in it a danger for German spiritual life. Gentz himself claims that his respect for Müller began with his hatred for Fichte.[10] Müller gladly allowed himself to be celebrated as the coming prophet, and he nourished the expectations with great intimations. His little book *Die Lehre vom Gegensatz*, which appeared in 1804, was, of course, a severe disappointment. The superficial and fragmentary manner in which he touched upon all the difficult problems of philosophy and the romantic combination of Goethe-Burke in which this philosophy culminated would inevitably have made a particularly bad impression on a knowledgeable person like Gentz, who was trained in the Kantian school. Notwithstanding all his enthusiasm for his friend, he was too clever not to see how meager the philosophy of polarity was, even though it had overpowered him to such an extent in sociable conversation and oratorical crinoline. He declared that he preferred any conversation with Müller to the book. The same disappointment was repeated after each of Müller's more comprehensive publications: after the appearance of the *Elemente der Staatskunst* (1809) and the *Versuche einer neuen Theorie des Geldes* (1816) (Essays on a new theory of money).This is why Gentz reserved his highest praise for the shorter essays: those that appeared in *Pallas*, the incidental piece on the return of the king of Prussia to Berlin in 1809, and also *Ueber die Notwendigkeit einer theologischen Grundlage der gesamten staatswissenschaften* (1819) (On the necessity of a theological basis for the political sciences), on which he wrote: "Unfortunately it is only a fragment. This fragment, however, contains paragraphs and passages that lie beyond comparison with anything in Germany, and in general it can be compared only with the best chapters of the immortal de Maistre. In many passages, even the style rises above what the best among us have accomplished."[11] Of course when one considers the striking effect of Müller's letters and the fine gestures with which he renounces the approbation of the world when it is denied him; when he proposes to put the incomprehension of the world to shame, if possible by means of even greater achievements; the calm superiority with which he declares the praise of a physician named Langermann to be more important than the praise of the world; when one sees how he already makes the romantic protest of the total work of art by representing his *Elemente der Staatskunst* as a new genre, a higher unity formed by the combination of philosophical, economic, and theological elements — a genre that, therefore, neither a philospher, nor an economist, nor a theologian is qualified to criticize — and when ever new promises and intimations appear in which a good friend would gladly put his trust, then it is understandable that even as late as 1823, Gentz was still capable of believing that Müller was the only person who would be able to do battle with Görres. Only now, he cautiously adds that it was "not without fear and trembling" that he would "see his friend go into this battle."

The empty *raison oratoire* that unrolls in a mechanical fashion, which Taine finds in the speeches of the Jacobins, cannot simply be equated with the oratorical accomplishments of Müller. That is because the latter exhibit a flourishing romantic productivity. And yet much of what Taine noted by way of characterizing the *raison oratoire* applies to a surprising extent here as well. "All this philosophy that is written has been spoken, and it has been spoken with accent, mood, and the inimitable simplicity of improvisation. . . . Everything there is arranged, studied . . . so that scarcely a fact and an instructive detail is recognized." There are few powerful passages in Müller's writings that he would not have found in earlier conversations or letters — for Müller, the letter was form of conversation too. After a reading of Kant's "Attempt to Incorporate the Concept of Negative Quantities into Conventional Wisdom," the claim that, for example. Fichte's nonego was the *nihil irrepraesentable* (the nonrepresentable nothing) was in itself not a profound assertion. A specialized philosophical term, which as such produced a certain esoteric effect, was projected into conversation. This made a powerful impression on Gentz, which can be gathered from his letter to Brinckmann.[12] But what a feeble effect the same passage produces in the larger context of the *Lehre vom Gegensatz,* and what cautious turns of phrase are brought into play against the dangerous opponent Fichte. And what a painful impression is produced by a practical detail in the *Elemente der Staatskunst.* After the conceited generalizations and mention of the idea, duration, and true statecraft, a small practical experiment is undertaken. To annul the laws of primogeniture, he claims, violates the existing legal order. But this is the true legal order because it is identical with true utility, and because I must respect "what the grandchildren among my contemporaries enjoy as an inheritance from their ancestors." As regards the annulment of common holdings among peasants, on the other hand, the matter is different. Why? "The evident increase in the pure revenue of a nation speaks in favor of the annulment. An ancient law speaks against it, however, a law that is much less comprehensive in its application than that which spoke against the annulment of primogeniture. Custom and the obstinacy of the peasant support the law. Here, nevertheless, immediate advantage can carry off the victory against a narrow-minded and weak law."[13] That is the entire argument. It is no wonder that Rehberg and Raumer, who were well versed in the practical difficulties of the question, scorned this as chatter and saw in it a cheap sophism that an orator served to his aristocratic patrons.

In addition to this aversion to concrete detail, which conformed to the ancient rhetorical principle that the orator is permitted to speak only in generalities, Müller had two other oratorical idiosyncrasies. They often appear so prominently in his expositions that the objective content disappears throughout extended passages. The first is his propensity for superlatives. Essentially an aftereffect of the Ciceronian tradition, in Müller it can be explained as a consequence of the fact that he deprives every pregnant word of its objective content. The word continues to figure as nothing more than an ornament. It is supposed to regain its impressive effect through superlative inflation. Just as the superlative appears with psychological necessity in conventional turns of speech and in the closing of letters (most humble, most cordial, most sincerely, obediently yours, most gracious), it dominates in many romantics because of a lack of substantive content and a "sociable" attitude. In the case of Müller, superlatives appear in enormous numbers. In the lectures and correspondence, there are often dozens. There are superlatives in which the thought could not achieve enough for itself with the mere affirmative, rotates in place, and heats itself up to the superlative. Where it would have sufficed to speak of the essence, in opposition to that which is inessential, the abstract idea attempts to make itself impressive by speaking of the inner essence, and finally of that most inner of all essences, obviously without enhancing the thought in this way. Fichte's work abounds with such incantations, such as "simply," "completely," "nothing but," "really," "purely," "only," "merely," "absolutely," "unconditionally." He knows, for example, "with absolute certainty," "that only by means of real, pure, and true thought, and simply by means of no other organ, can one grasp and bring to oneself the divinity and the blissful life that flows from it." In Fichte, this arises from the endeavor to force others to submit to his ideas. It was the despotic impulse for subjugation and the annihilating power of proof. In Müller, superlatives are only phonetic enhancements or rhetorical exclamation marks.

They are quite frequently linked with a second device that is also rhetorical: the three-part paraphrase. It could be called the Müller Ternary because it is so conspicuously predominant in his work. Here too, hundreds of examples can be given. "A beautiful, free, and vital life"; "gentleness, forbearance, and tolerance"; "censoriousness, intolerance, and unbelief"; "consumed, annihilated, and immolated by the flame of wit"; "in the highest, most earnest, and ardent devotion"; "the comical that is genuine, pure, and guileless"; "what is the holy of holies, what is the highest beauty, what is the purest truth if not . . ."; "the intense, free, and exuberant" (as a characteristic of the romantic); "the circumspect, elegant, and tactful" (as the mark of French classicism); "the innocence, abundance, and clarity of Homer"; "the finely drawn, arched, and polished loquacity of Cicero"; the "most agitated, sensitive, and soaring spirit of the ancient world" (Plato); and so on.[14] Sometimes this alternates with binary movements. It always remains, however, exclusively determined by rhythmic, acoustic, or other oratorical points of view, and it evolves over the years from a juvenile and awkward Ciceronian quality to a refined solemnity.

Müller's arguments can be judged only as an oratorical performance. The antitheses he expounds are not objective differences or oppositions, the superlatives are not substantive enhancements, and the "ternary" is not an accumulation of ideas, but rather of words. The antitheses are rhetorical. They are oratorical pendants, and with the help of rhythm and the effect of sonority, they can have a suggestive force. This is how the high-romantic assertion and blending of every imaginable "antithesis" are justified: man and woman, city and country, aristocracy and bourgeoisie, upper house and lower house, body and soul, person and thing, space and time, the subjective interior and the superficial exterior, past and future, the moment and permanence, right and utility, theory and practice, romantic and classical, Germanic and Roman, Orient and Occident, air and earth, and so on. They are interchanged. Sometimes they are treated as parallel contrasts, sometimes as antitheses, and sometimes as identities. They always remain mere sounds and chords that blend, contrast, or harmonize in accordance with the oratorical effect in a single case. Müller needs a dramatic image in order to illustrate the relationship between past and future, which for him is also nothing more than an image. Straightaway a new "antithesis" is produced: man and earth. The earth is the enemy of man. It destroys what he has built. The different human generations are allies in this war, after they had previously functioned as the antithesis between young and old. The private person, however, also wages a "war," with the state. Indeed, the wars of the Revolution and the Napoleonic Wars are "only a symbol" of this internal war that takes place in every state.[15] "War" prevails between private and public life, between property owners and the laws, between the shoemaker and the leather. Sometimes war is the father of all things. Sometimes it is evil. Sometimes the state must triumph in every battle with the private person. Sometimes the state itself is only the private person as conceived by Haller. This is all only *raison oratoire,* and it employs philosophy or political science only to the extent that is makes use of their terminology in the interests of a romantic productivity. In the review of the *Lehre vom Gegensatz* that appeared in 1805 in the *Jenaische Allgemeine Literaturzeiting* (Nr. 106, p. 238), it is correctly noted that a theory of polarity cannot do without the distinction between exclusive and nonexclusive antitheses. The author, however, was not concerned with elementary logical presuppositions of this sort. For him, the only thing that mattered was to speak and to float in the beautiful movement of a sociable conversation.

In addition, Müller cannot think at all unless it is in a conversation. The word *conversation* — the name for a special kind of romantic productivity that takes any object as the occasion for a sociable "play with words" — reappears unremittingly in his work. As early as the preface to the *Lehre vom Gegensatz*, he regrets that "no coherent conversation" is consummated "throughout Europe as a whole." This is repeated in all the editions. He cannot suppress it even in the memoir on the editing of a Prussian government newspaper: the government holds a "conversation" with the opposition. This manifests the romanticizing of the liberal "discussion" and "balance" and, at the same time, the liberal origins of this romanticism. This structure of Müller's intellectual productivity was already revealed in the *Lehre vom Gegensatz*. He explains that from the very beginning, every idea is construed as an opposition. In consequence, the antithesis is not merely a major figure of speech. On the contrary, "to the extent that it is completely vital, speech is utterly and endlessly antithetical." This is because "the listener is the true disputant" (p. 38). The speaker must conceive himself as listener, the listener as speaker. Both roles can be exchanged, like subject and object, positive and negative, and so on. This is the endless reciprocal interaction of which he continually speaks — and for Müller, this means whenever he wants to "grasp life in flight." It does not have an intellectual affinity with either Schelling or Bergson. On the contrary, it means that the antithetical quality of speech and objection is an occasion for the romantic experience. His main argument, which he asserts so frequently — in the beginning, there was not an individual person, but rather a community — means that for him, everything can become the occasion for a conversation. His refutation of the "celebrated misunderstanding of an absolute identity of subject and object" (p. 44) consists in the exemplification of a conversation, in which there must necessarily be two participants, the speaker and the listener. The One, therefore, is only a "constant Two."

The artist holds a conversation with the viewer of the artwork. And since nature and art are the same, nature also holds a conversation with the human being. Every flower and every picture becomes an interlocutor in a discussion, sometimes as listener and sometimes as speaker. The entire world, the universe, is a conversation. Thus occasionally the impression arises that this thought or feeling was sociologically oriented because — a rare case for a romantic — it has an appreciation for reciprocity and for the fact that the human being is not alone in the world. This human community, however, has only the romantic conversation as its content. In spite of his rejection of Schelling's system of identity — which, under these conditions, he could not understand — Müller adopted expressions and turns of phrase from Schelling as well as from numerous others. In this way, he concealed the subjective occasionalism of his cast of mind. It would be quite mistaken to speak of dualism or monism here, for in this context dualism and monism are not antitheses. That is because the antitheses themselves are not antitheses, but merely occasions. No concept retains its form. Everything dissolves into an oratorical music. The speaker can be imagined as being engaged in a "war" with the listener. He is just as much in a state of peace with the listener. Otherwise the conversation would not be possible. The antitheses are immediately mediated and reconciled, and an agreement invariably follows. The "community," which in fact is always assumed, is the immediate corporeal and spiritual proximity of friends and those of like mind. Here the "true" concept, in opposition to the false, can be spoken of unhesitatingly and without the necessity of entering into laborious conceptual or substantive demonstrations. In his addresses on rhetoric, Müller juxtaposed rhetoric as the masculine, which aims at activity and resolve, to poetry as the feminine. First of all, this is only a case of his oratorical contrasts; and it is virtually self-evident that, had his talent been poetic, he would have found something masculine in poetic production as a creative and generative activity, in opposition to rhetoric, which is functionally dependent upon a public. A touching lament, however, rings throughout the addresses. The Germans are a people who write, and thus they are a mute people[16] — the lament of the born speaker whose only great speeches are about rhetoric and whose talent, given the political conditions of the time, went no further than the modest heights of the eloquence of sociable gatherings and conversations among friends. The addresses are sustained by the longing for real political life. But they are only oratorical configurations of this longing to escape from the narrow confines of romantic empathy. Otherwise they contain literary criticism.

With the exception of the respects in which they merely contain paraphrases of ecclesiastical natural right, Friedrich Schlegel's endeavors in political philosophy are entirely lacking in political originality. Thus it is with reason that, where interests in literary history were not paramount, they have hardly been regarded as noteworthy in comparison with the publications of Adam Müller. But as long as even the most modest demands of objectivity and coherence are made, it is impossible to judge Müller's theory of the state as anything but a matter of aesthetics and style. Confused and without any instincts, he alters his view without the most elementary sense of consistency, though with splendid words about the necessity of his position. After every new impression, he inserts new heterogeneous elements into his productions and finds that he is invariably proven right, regardless of whether he — the "globular philosopher" of antitheses — is countered by Bonald, de Maistre, or Haller. In the *Elemente der Staatskunst*, it was with malicious scorn that he had abandoned the individualism of the eighteenth century to the liberal Prussian bureaucracy. Filled with enthusiasm, he had spoken of the state that demands everything — and, indeed, demands everything with love. It was only after reading Haller that he noticed what he could have already found in Burke: that this hyperbolic magnification of the state and this contempt for civil rights amounted to revolutionary Jacobinism. Now he employed the expedient — a beautiful example of romantic reversal — of declaring that every individual is the state. Now the state is composed of states, in conformity with the old individualistic conception of individuals. The objective of protecting the single individual from the despotism of the state — which earlier would have seemed to be a contemptible egoism — is achieved by virtue of the fact that the individual is also treated as the state. If for Haller all rights are civil rights, without there being a qualitative distinction between constitutional rights and civil rights, so for Müller all rights are constitutional rights: in other words, they are "really" civil rights as well. In the *Elemente der Staatskunst,* he had set out some vague reminiscences from the Nettelbladt school concerning the "positive" character of right — of course, deliberately belittling the "worthy man." Against natural right, he had claimed that everywhere there is a "locale," a positive instance that has its own intrinsic natural law. In other words, natural *right* is opposed to the "nature of the case."[17] For him, natural right was not natural enough. In other words, similar to the way Rousseau makes a concrete idyll out of nature, Müller makes nature into something that is concrete and poetic, the "locale." He had shown that he was incapable of any abstraction at all; for to him, every law whatever, and not merely natural right, was a lifeless word. That is because every concrete case is different from the law under which it is subsumed. Then in 1819, he identified his sensualism — which is manifested here in the incapacity for arriving at a logical concept and establishing a moral norm — with Haller's realism. At this point, he recognized the "right of the stronger" as the "natural" right, which could be set aside only by a theological natural right. In the *Theologische Grundlage,* however, not only are there approximations to Adam Smith — unexpectedly, Müller had again become an individualist. Rousseau's "tranquil peasant" also reappears, that is, what he had mentioned only as the "so-called" people in the articles by the "Correspondent from the South Tyrol," written in opposition to the demagogue Görres. De Maistre would have been the last person to have sympathy for this sort of romantic idea. And yet Müller believed himself to be in agreement with de Maistre: the incorrigible German sentimental pantheist, in his all-mediating sympathy for everything, in agreement with the profound skeptical pessimism of the diplomat without illusions and his principle that would inevitably destroy romanticism as a whole — namely, the view that man is evil in his volition and his impulses, and that he is good only by virtue of his intellect.[18] Müller's *Ueber die Notwendigkeit einer theologischen Grundlage der gesamten Staatswissenschaften* disintegrates into an oratorical figuration, formed from heterogenous material, of the following

quite insubstantial emotional judgment: The true state is the
true state.

There is no substantive or conceptual discussion that extri-
cates his account from the empty rounds of these affirmations
and negations. That is why it abounds in these synonyms for
the "true" and the "false": the vital, the genuine, natural, Christian, historical, and lasting, in opposition to the lifeless, mechanical, chimerical, hypocritical, pagan, and unnatural, and
in opposition to the surrogate (Müller was especially fond of
this word; Schlegel had already employed it against Kant, and
during the continental blockade, when ersatz tea, coffee, sugar,
and other commodities were encountered everywhere, it naturally came into general use), the caricature, the parody, the
bastard, and so on. These are the necessary trappings of romantic writing. They are protestations of emotional assent or
refusal, no more and no less than holds true for other paraphrases that seem to be more significant because of their philosophical associations, such as Müller's idea (= the true) and
concept (= the false), duration and the moment.

The thorough investigation of Adam Müller's theory of
money undertaken in Palyi's *Romantische Geldtheorie* [The romantic theory of money] arrives at the conclusion that Müller
quite often differed from "the political economy of his time
essentially only in the formal inversion of political economy,
but not by virtue of more profound insights." "Adam Müller
did not provide a more thorough development of the concept
of money in classical political economy, to say nothing of surmounting it. He made this concept indefinitely extensible, however, by means of an elastic use of language, to which he was
led by the romantic presuppositions of his thought; and in a
paradoxical fashion, he converted the traditional doctrine of
the relationship between the monetary and the nonmonetary
economic order into its opposite." This is the method natural
to romantic intellectualism. Müller picked up some interesting
details through the influence of Gentz, from his acquaintance
with experienced people such as Prussian landowners, and
especially in his work as an official. His article "The Bank of
London" in the *Shorter Brockhaus Encyclopedia* is actually a thoroughly matter-of-fact essay. In it, one of Müller's favorite im-

ages — centrifugal and centripetal force — does not serve as a rhetorical end in itself, but rather as the illustration for a substantive discussion. Here Müller is no longer romantic. The romantic theoretician — it is, of course, imprecise to speak of theory or thought in this context — lets the image do its own thinking. Abandoning himself to permutational or antithetical play with the ideas of others, he inflates linguistic designations of these ideas to an ambiguity rich in allusions. Thus there are no romantic ideas, but only romanticized ideas.

The occasional character of all romanticized objects

It is especially important for political romanticism that the intellectual material with which romantic affect seeks to shape itself is relatively indifferent. Not every affect produced by the political sphere needs to invest itself with political associations. In Novalis, we find the simplest examples of the fact that the occasional impression of a political object is transformed into oscillations of poetry and natural philosophy, and also of the fact that an unpolitical impression reverberates in political associations. The political is poeticized in aphorisms such as these: military decorations are wills-o'-the-wisp or shooting stars; soldiers have colorful uniforms because they are the pollen of the state; gold and silver are the blood of the state; the king is the sun of the solar system. This also holds for the numerous cases in which analogies from natural philosophy, theology, or some other "higher" science are brought into play. Here as well, the objective of elevating the object into a poetic sphere is decisive. The analogy does not serve the purpose of conceptual clarification or systematic or methodological inter- ests at all, which — unlike the romantics — is the case for true philosophers of nature, even when they are guilty of the crud- est misuse of such analogies. Proofs such as "the monarchy is the true system because it is connected at an absolute center" also appear in Bonald's work, where they express a Scholastic and systematic propensity for unity. In de Maistre, they would be the consequence of a specifically legalistic and extremely unromantic need for a final authority. In Novalis, they are aesthetically determined, and they are poetic figurations. This

is clearly manifested in fragments such as this: Hierarchy
is the "symmetrical root figure of the state, the principle of
state association as an intellectual perception of the political
ego." Here associations from the philosophy of nature, Fichte,
aesthetics, and politics are indiscriminately blended and foam
up in a rhythmically compact and substantively worthless
aphorism.

This romantic way of dealing with things is based on the
practice of constantly escaping from one sphere into another,
to the alien "higher" third factor, and of blending ideas from
different spheres. Solger's observation that in Adam Müller
everything is a "fraudulent adulteration" and Wilhelm Grimm's
trenchant remark that it is his sense that everything worthwhile
in Müller is "borrowed" point to the second principle: the use
of the ideas of others in this intermixture without any other
activity except that of literary exaggeration, which produces
paradoxical reversals as its consequence. The impression of
fraudulence is also brought about, however, by another factor
that stems from the intellectual distinctiveness of romanticizing. The point around which the circle of the romantic play of
forms turns is always occasional. Therefore, the romantic quasi
argument can justify every state of affairs. Today the centralized police state can be the lifeless, artificial machine to which
the vital energies of estatist privileges should not be sacrificed.
Tomorrow these privileges are proud flesh that must be restored to the vast living body as a whole. The separation of
powers can signify an artificial mutilation of the total organism.
And tomorrow it can signify a vital play of the antitheses that
recur in nature as a whole, antitheses in whose reciprocal interaction — because war is the father of all things — the living
organism is produced as a higher unity. Nothing is more unnatural and repellent than artificial "fabrication." It is revolutionary, and it does not last. The greatness of the Prussian
nation, however, is that it consciously creates what nature has
denied it. Today the French Revolution is what Burke thinks
it is: abnormal idolatry and a senseless crime. Tomorrow it can
also be "the natural force, the elective affinity of life oppressed
and in fetters," which breaks the bonds of moral considerations
and forms, and so on.[19]

Brief indication of the difference between political romanticism and a romantic politics: In the latter, it is the effect and not the cause that is occasional.

The lack of consistency and the moral helplessness in the face of each new impression have their basis in the essentially aesthetic productivity of the romantic. Politics is just as alien to him as ethics or logic. And yet the cases of political romanticism should probably be distinguished from another type, that of the romantic politician. A person who is not essentially a romantic can be motivated by romanticized ideas, and he can place his energy, which flows from other sources, at their disposal. In order to avoid discussing the involved and complicated actions of states, I shall consider the murder of Kotzebue by the student Karl Ludwig Sand as a paradigm of this sort of romantic politics.[20]

Sand was brought up in conformity with the moral strictness that still prevailed in the education of young people during the eighteenth century. As a boy and an adolescent, he tormented himself with a gymnastics of the will that was often pathetic, and he forced himself not to give way to any impulse of softness and lust. In France, where Robespierre provides a well-known example of this strict moralism, it would be characterized as an aftereffect of the strict tradition of the *esprit classique*. In Germany such a term would be misleading, since German classicism was already under the influence of humanitarian and Rousseauean ideas in which the earlier strictness was relaxed. It still existed in Germany, however, and in Sand it had the consequence that he retained the unromantic capacity for psychic innervation and the power of decision: the capacity for action in the usual, and not in the "higher," sense. As a student, he joined in the popular romanticism of his time, which was already idyllic. He was an enthusiast of old folk songs, and he glorified the Middle Ages with its authentic rectitude. He believed in his ideals of freedom and country without any romantic reservations. To this honorable man, Kotzebue — the old agent of Russia, greedy and malicious — appeared as the enemy. Primitive student politics, which was expressed in a dislike for the czar, had nothing specifically romantic about it. The direction of German patriotic feeling was consciously opposed only to all things French: to Gallicism, the enemy that had just been expelled and whose foreign rule had awakened the national consciousness. As a "Gallic," Kotzebue was "moral" only if this is meant to refer to his softness. In the main, the students regarded him as a "traitor" and a spy in the service of a political power that wanted to demoralize the spirit of the German student associations. It cannot be said, however, that Sand's decision was the result of a distinct national or political sentiment directed against an enemy that was clearly recognized. The act was certainly motivated by political ideas. But the fact that the choice fell directly on Kotzebue can very probably be explained by the consideration that for Sand, the "scoundrel" had become the symbol of baseness and vileness. He had become a romantic construct. This fact — Kotzebue's obvious political insignificance, which makes a murder and a crime into a foolish political incident — would still hold true even if Sand had acted on the basis of nothing but patriotic motives. The event acquires its romantic structure by virtue of the fact that a purely occasional object is imputed to an important political intent that is to be taken seriously. In this case, the structure is also occasionalistic because the point on which political energy concentrates is hit upon in an occasional fashion. It is only the direction that is externally oriented and opposed to political romanticism. Thus the effect, the *terminus ad quem,* is occasional. Not a *causa,* but rather an *effectus occasionalis* is present. A complex of powerful political energies is not able to find its objective, and it strikes an occasional point with great force.

The immortal type of this politics of romantically construed opportunities is Don Quixote, a romantic political figure, but not a political romantic. Instead of seeing the higher harmony, he was capable of seeing the difference between right and wrong and of making a decision in favor of what seemed right to him, a capacity that the political romantic lacks to such an extent that even the romantic legitimism of Schlegel and Müller has to be explained as a consequence of their indifference to justice. When enthusiasm for his ideal of chivalry and an indignation over supposed injustice drove the poor knight to a senseless disregard of external reality, still he did not withdraw aesthetically into his own subjectivity, composing complaints for a criticism of the present. His sincere zeal brought him into situations in which the romantic sense of superiority became impossible. His battles were fantastically absurd. But they were still battles in which he exposed himself to personal dangers, not battles of the higher sort like Adam Müller's battle of the artist with his material or the battle of the shoemaker with leather. He had the enthusiasm of a real knight for his rank, not the enthusiasm of a bourgeois for the impressive image of an aristocracy. In the nineteenth century, aristocratic romantics are romantic political figures rather than political romantics, and noblemen such as Arnim and Eichendorff (the latter, by the way, identified with Don Quixote) were never able to embody the type of the political romantic in the way that the bourgeois writers Schlegel and Müller did. Intimations of a new age in which ontology became a new problem, however, are evident even in Don Quixote. Here the Spanish nobleman often approximates a subjectivistic occasionalism. He declares his idea of Dulcinea to be more important than her real aspect. This is because who Dulcinea is does not matter. What matters is only that, for him, she remains the object of the ideal devotion that inspires him to great deeds (Book II, ch. 11; Book ix, ch. 15).

In the absence of the occasionalistic displacement into the higher, subjective creativity that resolves all antitheses in a harmonious unity, there is no romanticism. This is why the numerous historical parallels that characterize persons from ancient or medieval history as romantics — because of individual, and especially psychopathological, similarities — often employ the word only as a political figure of speech, as a synonym for vagueness, eccentricity, an overexcited frame of mind, or fanaticism. In that case, the vagueness of such a characterization is connected with the general uncertainty of historical analogies. Whoever draws a parallel between a Roman emperor and a ruler of the nineteenth century makes out of each a figure whose lines are often determined more by the constant regard for mutual similarity, which remained to be demonstrated, than by substantive investigations. Thus romantic characteristics can be ascribed to the emperor without taking into consideration the extent to which the romantic is something that is specifically modern. For example, when André Suarès makes an up-to-date configuration out of the Emperor Nero — whom he characterizes, with good psychological observations, as a tyrannical, capricious, coquettish mime — that is a kind of romantic artifact.[21] Historical parallels and comparisons of this sort are resources for literary composition. They like to employ as valuable motifs well-known historical persons and complexes that have already become mythological or legendary formulas and carry with them a cloud of emotional associations. Romantics such as Adam Müller or Benjamin Constant have made an Attila or a Genghis Khan out of Napoleon, and they have made use of these figures in the way that Novalis used Mary the Mother of God. This sort of romanticism does not involve any political activity. In conformity with its immanent presuppositions and methods, it intends an aesthetic effect. Consciously or unconsciously, it can serve political agitation, and it can have political effects without ceasing to be romantic — in other words, a product of political passivity — no more than Auber's *La Muette de Portici* became a political act or Auber became a politician by virtue of the fact that the enthusiasm of the revolutionaries was ignited by this opera during the Belgian revolution of 1830. The historical comparison that results from a political interest and is employed as a political means is different from this. One of the best known historical parallels that attempts to make a political type out of the romantic — David Friedrich Strauss's book *Julian the Apostate: The Romantic on the Throne of the Caesars* (Mannheim, 1847) — is based on such a topical political interest. It is of special importance for the conceptual scheme of *Political Romanticism.*

Excursus: the romantic as a political type in the conception of the liberal bourgeoisie, exemplified by David Friedrich Strauss's *Julian the Apostate*

David Friedrich Strauss wanted to controvert Wilhelm IV and his conservative and antiliberal policy by means of the comparison with Julian and the unsuccessful attempt to restore paganism in the fourth century A.D. In Julian's time, Christianity was the novel, the revolutionary, and the "spirit of the future" in opposition to the traditional pagan religion. In the nineteenth century, Christianity appears in a historically antiquated role, attempting to restore itself in opposition to a new life. David Friedrich Strauss's book discovers numerous analogies here, both in general and in particular: the attempts to raise the level of religiosity, to support schools and churches, and to attract philosophers to the court with the help of state institutions and measures; the reconstruction of temples or cathedrals; the belief in the religious mission of the ruler. These similarities, which are sketched with considerable skill, can appear not only in every restoration but also in a reformation. Harnack has characterized as an unprecedented innovation Julian's attempt to fill the cult, the cult community, and the priesthood with ascetic piety and to discipline them mystically and hierarchically[22] — an innovation that was partially realized only much later in the Christian Middle Ages by the popes who supported the Clunaic reforms, and that failed under Julian because the interests of the pagan mystery cults conflicted with those of the public state cult. Had the attempt succeeded, Harnack notes, the result would have been a reformation, not a reaction. But success cannot be the only thing that matters. Otherwise a successful undertaking would simply be a reformation, and an unsuccessful undertaking, romanticism.

In his book, Strauss provided a detailed definition of the concept of romanticism. "The historical situations in which romanticism and romantics can arise are epochs in which an antiquated culture confronts a new one. . . . At such watersheds of world history, persons in whom feeling and imagination outweigh clear thinking, spirits of more warmth than light, always turn backward, to what is old. From the unbelief and prose that they see gaining ground around them, they will long for the world of the old faith and ancestral customs, a world that is agreeable and rich in forms; and they will attempt to restore this world for its own sake and, wherever possible, beyond itself as well. But as children of their time, they too are dominated more than they know by the new principle that is repugnant to them. That is why the old ways as they are reproduced in and through them are no longer the pure and primordial old ways. On the contrary, they are blended in many respects with what is new, and in this way they reveal the new in advance. It is no longer a despotically proscribed faith that rules the subject, but rather a faith to which the subject willingly and deliberately clings. The good-natured consciousness conceals the contradiction and the falsehood that lie here by means of a fantastical obscurity in which it veils them: Romanticism is essentially mysticism, and only mystical spirits can be romantics. In part, however, the contradictions between the old and the new are quite evident, even in the deepest obscurity. In any case, the falsehood of a despotic faith must be felt in the innermost recesses of consciousness, which is why self-delusion and inner insincerity belong to the nature of all romanticism."

This definition — which was reproduced in detail because of its typical significance — probably best epitomizes a view of the romantic that is often repeated. In an interesting opposition to the Hegelians, it attempts to set up a general, world-historical type of the romantic, and it disregards the derivation from Protestantism, to which the Hegelians adhered. Strauss too perceives an inner insincerity and a subjective tyranny in the romantic. He explains it, not incorrectly, in terms of the inner uncertainty in a conflict between antagonistic forces. Subjectivism seems to him to be a consequence, however, and not the cause, of the conflicting romantic phenomena. In the ensuing discussion, in the description of Julian's moral and intellectual qualities — which always alludes to the political romanticism of the time — the external symptoms that are perceived as romantic stand out in a pronounced fashion. What is specifically mentioned here — Julian's nervousness, his inclination to effusions of feeling, his coquettish pleasure in witty remarks, his need to give speeches or write letters to friends at every opportunity, his premeditation and affection — is interesting for knowledge of the portrait that was made of a romantic in 1848. This portrait is also well executed. But it is not sufficient to ground a pregnant concept of the romantic, and least of all as this concept applies to a man such as Julian who, with ascetic severity, endeavored to realize in practice the ancient ideal of virtue based on justice and intelligent moderation. The substantive elements of the definition, however, are disparate. Mysticism, which exists only in the domain of the religious, is thrown together with romanticism, which belongs essentially to the aesthetic. Since this is an old mistake, it need not surprise anyone. In its encounter with the opposition between the old and the young, however, it is altogether inexplicable why mysticism, which is supposed to be an essential part of the romantic, develops such a contradictory and untruthful product as the romantic. Nor is it probable that a person in whom feeling and imagination outweigh clear thought will give preference to the old existing state of affairs. And in conflicts between the old and the young, rationalism is not self-evidently on the side of the young.

Objections of this sort, however, should not be raised against Strauss's definition. That is because it only apparently sets out the elements of the romantic in a conceptual fashion. In fact, it is a quick typification of the actual current political opponent. At this point, shortly before 1848, the political program defines the concept even more clearly than was the case in Ruge (1840): Whoever is not progressive is a romantic. The feeling of representing the coming, new age is certain and self-evident. The opponent's political view appears so fundamentally incomprehensible that his opposition can be explained only as a consequence of inner insincerity and caprice. Again, the apparently unavoidable error is committed. Instead of the romantic subject, the occasional theme of romantic productivity is considered; instead of the process of romanticizing, one of the many romanticized contents, the result of this process. As a result, Strauss arrives at a clear disregard of obvious contradictions. He sets out in detail how Julian, in an extremely unclear fashion and with the help of vague interpretations, proposed to resuscitate the old pagan gods; and he points out the connection between Neoplatonic mysticism and Schelling's philosophy of nature. He draws our attention to Creuzer's symbolism and its philosophical transformation of all the concepts of Christian theology, which has its counterpart in the Neoplatonic transformation of the pagan Olympus. It might have occurred to him, however, that the mystical elucidation was certainly man-

ifested in liberals such as Oken and — even with the entire
force of immediate, subjective, inner conviction — in democratic advocates of German student associations, in Karl Follen
and his adherents; the development of the reactionary, so-
called political romanticism, on the other hand, had long since
led to a contrary standpoint.

German romanticism began as a youth movement, and as
long as it was really blended with the philosophy of nature and
with mysticism, it assumed a revolutionary posture. When it
joined with the political reaction, it embraced a strict, positive
orthodoxy that rejected that elucidation of Christian ideas as
"atheism" and a "fraud of the philosophy of nature." Jarcke
was anything but a romantic. And yet the liberals regarded
him as a romantic because he put himself at the disposal of
Metternich. This was the case even though Jarcke, as an intelligent and serious man, regarded the romanticism of the Vi-
ennese Biedermeier era as "empty and dissolute, and
unchristian in its innermost nature," and even though he provided a classical account of the horror of a subjectivistic mysticism with his description of "scenes of horror in
Wildenspuch." Haller was neither a romantic nor a mystical
symbolist. And throughout liberal and reactionary Germany,
there was probably no one who was as frankly contemptuous
of pantheistic-mystic theologians as de Maistre — who, in addition, saw Julian as one of "those dangerous dreamers" and
a "philosoph." Therefore, it is not necessary to consider in any
more detail the factions that are at stake here. That is because
the "old" and the "new" are a characterization that can itself
be called romantic when it is alleged to have the value of an
independent argument.

Early romanticism believed itself to be a new and — precisely
for that reason — more worthy age. In Novalis, we hear the
repeated claim that now a new era is dawning that will accomplish what "heretofore" was not possible. At that time, therefore, the "new" still belonged in the positive list of romantic
quasi argumentation. The new was life — organic, genuine,
and so on. As the romantics grew older, the dignity of the old
revealed itself to them. Now the old = the permanent = the
genuine = the organic = life, and so on. As regards the actual

contemporary circumstances of Strauss's book, the factions are not precisely designated. Both a political and an intellectual antagonism seem to be at issue. The fact that he compares Julian with Friedrich Wilhelm IV of Prussia could indicate the political character of the struggle between the old and the new. But it is obvious that the political and the intellectual cannot be so rigorously distinguished here. That is because the new scientific attitude defended by Strauss considered itself to be on the side of the opponents of the old. And, conversely, Friedrich Wilhelm IV conceived his policy as a religious and intellectual matter. Among the philosophers of the restoration, we repeatedly find the view that the French Revolution was the consequence of an unchristian philosophy of the Enlightenment, and that the battle against an idea, against paganism and ungodliness, must be carried on.

In spite of this, the state and society were the real object of the struggle. The restoration was a composite of political and social forces that were directed against a political and social opponent. The religious life that spontaneously sprang up among Catholics and Protestants in Germany after the Napoleonic Wars had developed independently of political measures. It was only used for political purposes. The agents of the Church, who, of course, collaborated with the political restoration to a great extent, placed themselves at its disposal because of their historical association with a specific political and social order. They were not the political leaders, however. Finally, the intellectual productivity that is linked with the restoration is essentially a product of political philosophy. Systems developed with ideas of social solidarity that can be characterized as just as new as those of liberal individualism. The antithesis with which Bonald begins and ends his *Théorie du pouvoir* (1796), and with which he gives an account of the theme of conflict, is not religious, but political and social. "The great question that divides men and societies in Europe is this: Man makes himself and he makes society; society makes itself and it makes man." And Bonald prides himself on having reduced this question from the level of philosophical fantasies and speculations to that of facts. When the theoreticians of the restoration reproach their opponents with the charge of atheism, a theological concept becomes a political concept. For Comte's positivism, Christianity had been superseded, and it is well known that Taine and Renan regarded Christianity as a product of a decadent culture. But because they arrived at a rejection and a repudiation of the French Revolution, today French royalists, the successors of Bonald and de Maistre, appeal to Comte, Taine, and even Renan, and call themselves, together with the last three named, realists. The criterion is precisely of a political nature.

In contrast to the restoration of 1815, the story of Julian is only the history of an unsuccessful cult reform and the inner mission of paganism. It is not the history of a political endeavor. Because it emanated from the emperor, the enterprise was supported by the instruments of state power, without thereby amounting to more than the love affair of a theosoph, cunning on the throne and otherwise capable in practical matters. It was not a movement that had its source in paganism. Athanasius called it a "cloudlet." A modern Prussian historian who compares Julian with Frederick II and defends him as a champion of the state fighting against ecclesiastical intolerance, O. Gruppe, calls it "a symbolic accident."[23] Negri holds, probably correctly, that Julian was neither a reactionary nor an advocate of Enlightenment.[24] He believed in the Neoplatonic doctrine, which to him was more a religion than a philosophy, and as a soldier he was influenced by the cult of Mithras. Christianity did not confront him as a political enemy. It did not pose an immediate threat to the existence of the empire in the way that the revolution of the eighteenth century threatened the existing state order. When Julian reproaches the Christians with "atheism," this is not, as was the case earlier in the period of the imperators, virtually a concept of criminal law, but rather an expression of the conviction of the emperor that the God of the Christians is not the true God. Julian's argument conforms to this position. It searches out contradictions in the doctrines of the Christians, makes moral reproaches against them, and opposes them by means of a polytheism transfigured by Neoplatonic ideas.

In the nineteenth century, the Christian churches were united with the existing political and legal order in the struggle against the revolutionary doctrine, and arguments against Christianity could be expected from Julian, the advocate of paganism united with the state, similar to those that legitimist philosophers advanced against revolution. This holds true, however, only for particulars. In the Hellenist and the Neoplatonic esoteric — whose religious and political endeavors were concerned only with the sophists of Athens and Antioch, but hardly with the genuine pagan traditions that still persisted in Roman senatorial families — there is nothing of the idea that religion, like language, is a constitutive element of every extensive human community, the traditional idea that God reveals himself in the community as such. The reason for this is that he was too occupied with the content of a specific religious and philosophical conviction. Of course, as Strauss particularly stresses, he also brings out the allusion to tradition and duration that is natural to the conservative position. Pagan polytheism is the old and the established, the religion that made the Roman state great. Christianity, on the other hand, is an absurd innovation without any relation to political life and with a kind of love of one's fellow man that will inevitably break up the state. He founds his pontificate on tradition, and he looks after the preservation of the ancestral laws. He also connects this with the ancient doctrine of the divine origin of the laws. And yet for Julian, this signifies a reiteration of Neoplatonic ideas, and at times also a moral indignation over the ungodliness of the Christians. But it is always the expression of his purely metaphysical belief in the connection between religion and fate, in the protection of the gods and the efficacy of prayer. For numerous metaphysical reasons, the God of the Galileans is not the true God. Therefore, he cannot help us. This is the cardinal point of his argument. Often this personal piety in fact calls to mind pious phrases from the romantics that were of service to the political restoration. In the case of Julian, however, the issue concerns a "counterreligion," not a counterrevolution. A church with the claim to absolute truth — when it became the established Church, it abolished the traditional, relativistic tolerance for all divinities and all confessions practiced by the state of classical antiquity — confronted a state that, in the imagination of the time, embraced the entire earth. The contradiction in Julian's situation did not result from subjectivistic caprice, but rather from this circumstance. Even if his personal convictions had been different, he still had to confront his religious opponent on religious grounds. A pagan religion that was also absolutely true had to meet the demand of the absolute religion of Christianity, even though the nature and the political value of this polytheism consisted precisely in its religious relativity.

As soon as the liberal Strauss approaches this aspect of Julian's reform work in his book, he makes a striking about-face. Now the reactionary emperor suddenly seems to him to be an intelligent and even likable man. That is because here he appeared not merely as a "romantic," but also as a *pagan* romantic," which means that he "differs" from the Christian romantics. "Or rather (!) he appears in opposition to them in a way that could hardly turn out to his disadvantage" (p. 47). Had Strauss been more clearly aware of the extent to which Julian's religious policy conforms to the liberal idea that every religion must be tolerated in the state, he surely would have refused — just as resolutely as O. Gruppe did — to speak of romanticism here at all. For a quick apprehension of the difference between Julian's arguments and those of restoration romanticism, we need only clear up what the factions really were that confronted one another as the old and the new in this case. The emperor confronted his enemy, a religious belief, with religious arguments. The theologizing romantic withdrew from a political discussion into religious demonstrations. Theology served him as a romantic alibi. This was political romanticism. But it was romanticism just as much as the romanticizing of the Revolution or of Napoleon, in which the followers of Strauss, the new romantic generation, indulged. In particular, Bettina von Arnim now became a revolutionary again. In 1843, she published *Dies Buch gehört dem König* [This book belongs to the King] and in 1851 *Gespräche mit Dämonen* [Conversations with Demons], typical products of revolutionary political romanticism.

Conclusion: political romanticism as the concomitant emotive response to political events

Wherever a serious political interest confronts political romanticism, either the latter is placed at the disposal of politics as a welcome medium of political suggestions, or moral reproaches are made against the inner "untruthfulness" of the romantic. Every political activity — regardless of whether its content is merely the technique of conquest, the claim or the expansion of political power, or whether it rests on a legal or a moral decision — conflicts with the essentially aesthetic nature of the romantic. A person of political or moral energy quickly perceives the substitution of categories and knows how to distinguish the romantic interest in a thing from the thing itself. Because the concrete point around which the romantic novel develops is always merely occasional, everything can become romantic. In such a world, all political or religious distinctions are dissolved into an interesting ambiguity. The king is a romantic figure as well as the anarchist conspirator, and the caliph of Baghdad is no less romantic than the patriarch of Jerusalem. Here everything can be substituted for everything else.

Under the impression of the lack of objectivity that a romantic treatment of political questions easily evokes in an honest opponent, it is especially opponents of Adam Müller, such as Rehberg and Solger, who called him a sophist. The word has a positive sense. It is not simply an empty term of abuse. That is because the connection between subjectivism and sensualism that is exhibited in Greek sophistry also nullified all objectivity and made substantive argument into a capricious productivity of the subject. The orator felt no other sense of responsibility than that of speaking well, and he knew no other satisfaction than the pleasure taken in the well-executed, artistic form of his speech. For example, in the letters of Libanius, Julian's teacher, this completely amoral and natural enjoyment of his own oratorical achievement is expressed in similes, in which he says that he speaks like the bird sings and has no other wish than to sing like the nightingale.[25] Even though the aestheticism of these Sophists provides the basis for many similarities with romantic productivity, they still lack what is specifically romantic: the occasionalistic displacement into a "higher third" sphere that leads the romantic into mysticism or theology, the secularization of God into the genial subject, who is not satisfied with a formal perfection even in art, but instead employs forms in an arbitrary and occasional fashion in order to find the higher meaning and a metaphysical or cosmic resonance for his subjective experience. The essential contradiction of the romantic — which, especially in political romanticism, justifies the impression of inner untruthfulness — is that the romantic, in the organic passivity that belongs to his occasionalist structure, wants to be productive without becoming active.

This remains the core of political romanticism. As subjectified occasionalism, it did not have the power — even in relation to itself and in spite of numerous psychological refinements and confessional subtleties — to objectify its intellectual nature in a theoretical or practical-substantive connection. Its subjectivism directed it, not to concepts and philosophical systems, but rather to a kind of lyrical paraphrase of experience. The latter could be combined with that organic passivity. Or, where artistic talent is lacking, it is linked with the half lyrical, half intellectualistic accompaniment of the activity of another person described above, following political events with marginal character glosses, catch phrases, viewpoints, emphases and antitheses, allusions and permutational comparisons, often agitated and excited, but always without making its own decision and assuming its own responsibility and risk. Political activity is not possible in this way. But criticism is, which can discuss everything and inflate it ideologically, revolution as well as restoration, war and peace, nationalism and internationalism, imperialism and its renunciation. Here as well, its method was the occasionalist departure from the domain to which the disputed opposition belongs, from the domain of the political into the higher domain. During the restoration, that meant an occasionalist departure into the domain of the religious. The result: absolute governmentalism; in other words, absolute passivity. The outcome: a lyrical and discursive tremolo of ideas that sprang from the decision and the responsibility of others.

Where political activity begins, political romanticism ends, and
it is no contradiction and no accident that the successors of
Bonald and de Maistre, the politically active royalists of the
Third Republic, derided the revolutionary ideology of the liberal bourgeois as romanticism with the same determination that
the liberal German bourgeois — when he made an attempt to
become politically active — discovered the romantic in his reactionary brother. In the nineteenth century, both bourgeois
revolutionaries and bourgeois reactionaries have a romanticism
alongside them as a companion, like a colorful moving shadow.

Political romanticism is a concomitant emotive response of
the romantic to a political event. This political event evokes a
romantic productivity in an occasional fashion. An impression
suggested by historical and political reality is supposed to become the occasion for subjective creativity. When the subject
lacks real aesthetic — in other words, lyrical-musical — productivity, an argument develops out of historical, philosophical,
theological, or some other scientific material, an intellectual
music for a political program. This is not the irrationality of
myth. That is because the creation of a political or a historical
myth arises from political activity, and the fabric of reasons,
which myth cannot forgo either, is the emanation of a political
energy. A myth arises only in the real war. Romantic activity,
however, is a contradiction in terms. Romanticism not only
lacks the specific connection with the restoration, which erro-
neous German linguistic usage designates "political romanticism"; it has no necessary relationship to revolution either. The
isolated and absolute ego is elevated above both and uses both
as an occasion. One should not be misled by an unclear terminology from literary history — a terminology that is itself
also influenced by romanticism — to confuse the pretentious
expansion of the aesthetic, which the romantic movement is
based on, with political energy; no more than one should,
conversely, make the incidental feature most noteworthy in the
everyday political polemics of the German reactionary period,
the connection with the Catholic restoration (at that time, the
strongest power), into the definitive criterion. It is also inac-
curate to situate the "excessive individualism" of which Seillière
and the other French speak in the subjectivistic elements of

the romantic. Here individualism has a sense only if the word retains a moral meaning as the antithesis of what is collective or social, and only if it designates the autonomous in opposition to the heteronomous. There is, to be sure, a connection with the autonomy of the individual. By virtue of the displacement into the domain of the aesthetic, however, the concept of autonomy, which is essentially moral, is completely changed, and all such distinctions are dissolved. In every romantic, we can find examples of anarchistic self-confidence as well as an excessive need for sociability. He is just as easily moved by altruistic feelings, by pity and sympathy, as by presumptuous snobbery.

But all this has nothing to do with either autonomy or heteronomy, and it moves entirely within the sphere of romantic subjectivity. An emotion that does not transcend the limits of the subjective cannot be the foundation of a community. The intoxication of sociability is not a basis of a lasting association. Irony and intrigue are not points of social crystallization; and no societal order can be established on the basis of the need, not to be alone, but rather to be suspended in the dynamic of an animated conversation. This is because no society can discover an order without a concept of what is normal and what is right. Conceptually, the normal is unromantic because every norm destroys the occasional license of the romantic. In the face of a normative concept, even the romantic qualities of antithesis and contrast break down. The courage of a brave man is not the higher unity formed from depression and exaltation. The rationally ordered state is not a synthesis of anarchy and despotism. As such, legal ideas are unromantic in the same way. Viewed romantically, injustice is only a dissonance that is aesthetically resolved "in a sacred music, an endless feeling of the higher life." This is not spoken in a metaphorical sense, but rather in the only category that is accessible to the experience of the romantic. That is why there is neither a romantic law nor a romantic ethics, just as it would be confused to speak of a lyrical or a musical ethics. There is a political romanticism in the same sense that there is a political lyric.

Thus the riotous disorder of the romantic is reduced to its simple principle of a subjectified occasionalism, and the mysterious contradiction of the diverse political tendencies of so-called political romanticism is explained as a consequence of the moral deficiency of a lyricism that can take any content at all as the occasion for aesthetic interest. The question of whether monarchist or democratic, conservative or revolutionary ideas are romanticized is irrelevant to the nature of the romantic. They signify only occasional points of departure for the romantic productivity of the creative ego. The core of this fantastic superiority of the subject conceals, however, the renunciation of every active alteration of the real world, a passivism whose consequence is that henceforth, romanticism itself is employed as an expedient of unromantic activity. In spite of its subjective superiority, ultimately romanticism is only the concomitant of the active tendencies of its time and its environment. Rousseau's historical significance is that he romanticized concepts and arguments of the eighteenth century; his lyricism worked to the benefit of the Revolution, the victorious movement of his time. German romanticism first romanticized the Revolution, and then the dominant restoration. After 1830, it again became revolutionary. In spite of irony and paradox, a consistent dependence is manifest. In the most limited area of its distinctive productivity, in lyrical and musical poetry, subjective occasionalism may discover a small island of free creativity. But even here it unconsciously submits to the strongest and most proximate power. And its superiority over the present, which is taken in a purely occasional fashion, undergoes an extremely ironical reversal: Everything that is romantic is at the disposal of other energies that are unromantic, and the sublime elevation above definition and decision is transformed into a subservient attendance upon alien power and alien decision.

Notes

Preface

1. Giovanni Papini, *Il crepuscolo dei filosofi*, 56.

2. Donoso Cortés, *El clasicismo y el romanticismo*, II, 5–41 (this first appeared in 1858 in the *Correo Nacional*).

3. G. A. Borgese, *Storia della critica romantica in Italia* (Milan, 1924), 193ff.

4. K. E. Lusser, *Hochland*, May 1924. See especially p. 177. See also Kathleen Murray, *Taine und die englische Romantik* (Munich and Leipzig: Duncker and Humblot, 1924), introduction.

5. Kathleen Murray, *Taine und die englische Romantik*, 55f.

Introduction

1. Arnold Ruge in his essay "Das Manifest der Philosophie und seine Gegner," 1840 (*Gesammelte Schriften*, III, Mannheim, 1846, 167).

2. See the essay "Friedrich von Gentz und das Prinzip der Genusssucht," in Ruge and Echtermeyer, eds., *Hallische Jahrbücher* (1839), 281ff. See also Ruge, *Friedrich Gentz und die politische Konsequenz der Romantik* (*Gesammelte Schriften*, I, 432–530).

3. Friedrich Karl Wittichen, ed., *Briefe von und an Friedrich von Gentz* (Munich and Berlin, 1909-).

4. Friedrich Karl Wittichen, *Mitteilungen des Instituts für österreichische Geschichtsforschung* 50 (1910), 110.

5. Victor Klemperer, *Romantik und französische Romantik: Festschrift für Karl Vossler* (Heidelberg, 1922), 27.

6. Georg von Below, *Die deutsche Geschichtsschreibung von den Freiheitskriegen bis zu unsern Tagen*, 2d ed. (Munich and Leipzig, 1924), 4, with reference to M. Lenz, *Jahrbuch der Goethe-Gesellschaft* II (1915), 299.

7. Arnold Ruge, *Die wahre Romantik: ein Gegenmanifest (Gesammelte Schriften*, III, 134). Thus romanticism is a longing. Even the longing to get over romanticism is still romanticism; the wish to enjoy freedom as fully as possible, "this most secret love-affair of our anxious age."

8. Karl Marx, *Die Helige Familie* (Frankfurt am Main, 1845), 19. The criticism that Marx raised in the *Deutsch-Französische Jahrbücher* is well known. The following sentence from a letter by Engels of September 28, 1892 (reported by Franz Mehring in *Die Lessing-Legende*, Stuttgart, 1893, 440), is of special interest. "During his Bonn and Berlin period, Marx had become acquainted with the restoration of Adam Müller and Herr von Haller. He spoke of this jejune, long-winded, and inflated imitation of the French romantics Joseph de Maistre and Cardinal Boland (he means Bonald) only with considerable contempt." In the essay on Hegel's *Philosophy of Right*, Marx does not use the expression 'romanticism.' In *The Poverty of Philosophy* (1847, 116–17), on the other hand, he says that fatalistic economists are either classical or romantic. The classicists look upon development with a blasé lack of pity. The romantics are humanitarian and advise the impoverished proletarians to be frugal, and so on. Here the French usage is clear: romantic = humanitarian.

9. F. Brunetière, "Le mouvement littéraire au XIX. siècle," *Revue des deux mondes*, October 15, 1889, 874. . . .

10. Friedrich Meinecke, *Weltbürgertum und Nationalstaat: Studien zur Genesis des deutschen Nationalstaats*, 6th ed. (Munich and Berlin, 1922), chapters IV, V, and VII.

11. Georg von Below, *Die deutsche Geschichtsschreibung*, 9.

12. Victor Klemperer, *Romantik und französische Romantik*. . . .

13. Vladimir G. Simkhovitch, *Marxismus gegen Sozialismus*, (Jena, 1913), 26–27.

14. Paléologue, *Romantisme et Diplomatie: Talleyrand, Metternich, Chateaubriand* (Paris, 1924), 101ff. It does not have to be said that Talleyrand and Metternich were not romantics (Paléologue also speaks only of the "romantic legend of diplomacy"). They were no more romantics than countless other figures who served as the occasion for romantic productivity. Even though George Sand's literary exaggerations blow up Talleyrand into a romantic and a demonic figure, historically he remains what he is: a brilliant technician of cabinet politics.

Chapter 1

1. Adam Müller, letter of January 13, 1825, from Leipzig, *Briefwechsel*, Nr. 219.

2. See Gunnar Rexius, "Studien zur Staatslehre der historischen Schule," *Historische Zeitschrift* 107 (1911), 506, where he stresses the importance of the English influence for the empirical tendency in German jurisprudence and historical science.

3. *Briefwechsel Gentz-Müller* (Stuttgart, 1857), Nr. 93, May 28, 1808.

4. Franz Rühl, ed., *Briefe und Aktenstücke aus dem Nachlass von Stägemann*, I (Leipzig, 1899), 118.

5. See Solger's *Nachgelassene Schriften*, I (Leipzig, 1826), 205. The letter to Raumer of December 2, 1810, is also in F. Raumer, *Lebenserinnerungen*, I, 227–28. For Wilhelm Grimm, see Steig, "Kleists Berliner Kämpfe," 505–506 *(Frankfurter Zeitung*, June 12, 1914), and Wilhelm Grimm's letter to his brother of October 5, 1809. In the correspondence of Rahel and Alexander von der Marwitz, see the latter's letters of May 26 and June 1 and 9, 1811. The citations can be easily multiplied.

6. *Briefwechsel Gentz-Müller*, Müller's letters of February 7, 1814, and September 30, 1814 (Nr. 118 and Nr. 120).

Chapter 2

1. Christian Janentzky, *Mystik und Rationalismus* (Munich and Leipzig, 1922), 9. See also the extraordinarily clear essay by Erik Peterson, "Zur Theorie der Mystik," *Zeitschrift für systematische Theologie* I, 165. Mysticism exists only "in the domain of" religion . . . "insofar as mysticism is ontically linked with the religious world."

2. Siegbert Elkuss, "Zur Beurteilung der Romantik and zur Kritik ihrer Forschung," *Historische Bibliothek* 39 (1918), 32. This important and uncommonly rich treatise has, unfortunately, remained a fragment.

3. The romantic elements are not decisive for Burke's political view. They mediated the great impact on romanticism, and thus the reception of conservative ideas as well. I did not emphasize this point sufficiently in the first edition, and in this regard I am indebted to M.J. Bonn's essay on Burke *(Frankfurter Zeitung*, July 10 and 12, 1897), which I did not become acquainted with until later, for an important suggestion. Burke's aesthetics is also of great interest here. In his work, the dark appears as the new sign of the sublime; music appears as the example of *pulchritudo vaga*, of free beauty in opposition to beauty that adheres to an object; and so on. See the Strassburg dissertation of Candrea, 1894. Siegbert Elkuss ("Zur Beurteilung der Romantik," 11) has provided an accurate summary of Burke's complex significance. The stream of ideas that flows from Burke divides into the historical conception of the world and political romanticism in the strict sense. In Burke, both are united. In Burke, the Enlightenment, the Reformation, and revolution as individualistic and rationalistic movements are also juxtaposed to traditionalism.

4. Aulard, *Histoire politique de la révolution francaise*, 367. . . .

5. Bonald, *De la philosophie moral et politique du 18. siècle* (October 6, 1805), published in *Mélanges littéraires, politiques et philosophiques*, I (Paris, 1819), *Oeuvres*, X, 104–133. See also III, 388f. . . .

6. Bonald, *Théorie du pouvoir* (1796); *Essai analytique sur les lois naturelles de l'ordre social*, *Oeuvres*, I (Paris, 1817), 307n. 1: La réalité est dans l'histoire, il ne considère pas la société. See also III, 213.

7. De Maistre, *Considérations sur la France* (1796); *Essai sur le principe générateur des constitutions politiques* (Paris, 1814, written in 1809), Nr. XLVII and XL. . . .

8. Bonald, *Oeuvres*, I, 193. . . .

9. Bodin, *Republik*, C.V., c. 1, "des moyens de connaître le naturel des peuples." Because of the astrological language in which Bodin often discusses these questions, I should like to add an observation here. Even good historians overlook the extent to which many allegedly new ideas are articulated by authors of the Middle Ages and the sixteenth and seventeenth centuries in astrological idioms that are obsolete today. The point that every people and every country has its own special character to which laws and customs conform certainly did not remain concealed from these times. They only formulate it in such a way that they speak of the distinctive genius, the special planet or constellation of the people or country. This was a commonplace idea, and thoroughly banal scribblers of the seventeenth century, such as Christoph Besold, composed writings on the special nature and genius of the different peoples and their varied laws and customs.

10. In the cases of Stourdzas and Baader, it is clear that the Greek Orthodox church could have the same effect as the Roman Catholic church. Had Schlegel gone to Russia — which he would have done if "a truly excellent and splendid position" had been provided for him there (letter to August Wilhelm of January 16, 1813, in Oskar F. Walzel, ed., *Friedrich Schlegels Briefe an seinen Bruder August Wilhelm*, Berlin, 1890, 537) — the result probably would have been similar to the case of Baader. See his *Philosophie der Geschichte*, 2 vols. (Vienna, 1829), 270ff. There was another resolution of the romantic situation, which the only great figure among the romantics (for I do not consider Kleist a romantic) met with: Kierkegaard. In Kierkegaard, all the elements of the romantic were in force: irony; the aesthetic conception of the world; the antitheses of the possible and the real, the infinite and the finite; the feeling for the concrete moment. His Protestant Christianity made him into the only individual who exists in the God of Christianity. In the immediacy of the relationship to God, every intrinsically worthy community was abolished. For political romanticism, this solution does not come into consideration.

11. *Blütenstaub*, Fragment 2 (Minor II, 11). "A word of command," this passage continues, "moves armies."

12. Oskar F. Walzel, ed., *Friedrich Schlegels Briefe an seinen Bruder*, 32.

13. Sainte-Beuve, *Port-Royal*, V, 237.

14. Malebranche, *Recherche de la vérité*, 1, II, Part 3, chapter IV, De l'imagination de Sénèque.

15. Malebranche, *Recherche*, Eclaircissement IX.

16. See Adam Müller, *Vermischte Schriften*, I, 81.

17. Adam Müller, "Die innere Staatshaushaltung systematisch dargestellt auf theologischer Grundlage, Erster Versuch," *Concordia*, Nr. 2 (Vienna, 1820), 87ff. (*Gesammelte Schriften*, 263ff).

18. See Adam Müller, *Elemente der Staatskunst*, II, 249.

19. Adam Müller, *Elemente der Staatskunst*, I, 66.

20. W. Metzger, *Gesellschaft, Recht, und Staat in der Ethik des deutschen Idealismus* (1917), 258.

Chapter 3

1. J. Lupus, *Le traditionalisme*, II (Liege, 1858), 58.

2. Bonald, *Oeuvres*, III, 367.

3. Bonald, *Essai analytique, Oeuvres*, I, 167.

4. Bonald, *Pensées diverses* (1817), *Oeuvres*, V, 52.

5. Gentz, *Historische Journal*, II, 48–49.

6. Adam Müller, *Briefwechsel*, Nr. 50–51.

7. See p. 46, above.

8. Freidrich Schlegel, *Briefe an seinen Bruder*, 17, 401. On August 26, 1791 (17): "The whole subject interests me chiefly in an indirect way, namely, as a vehicle for conversation with a great many people."

9. Novalis, *Monologen* 1 (Minor II, 18–19).

10. *Briefe von und an Friedrich von Gentz*, II, April 26, 1803, 125.

11. Gentz, *Briefwechsel*, letter of January 2, 1823 (Nr. 218).

12. *Briefe von und an Friedrich von Gentz*, II, April 26, 1803, 125.

13. Adam Müller, *Elemente der Staatskunst*, I, 89–90. See also *Friedrich II*, 99, and *Deutsche Staatsanzeigen*, II, 53.

14. The examples cited here are taken from the fourth, fifth, and sixth issues of *Phoebus*. See Adam Müller, *Vermischte Schriften*, II, 165, 214ff.

15. Adam Müller, *Friedrich II*, 27.

16. Adam Müller, *Zwölf Reden über die Beredsamkeit und deren Verfall in Deutschland, gehalten zu Wien im Frühling 1812* (Leipzig, 1816). Here the antipathy against German writing and publishing has a tone of aristocratic superiority. This was a gesture that he borrowed from people like Steigentesch.

17. Adam Müller, *Elemente der Staatskunst*, I, 57–59.

18. De Maistre, *Du Pape*, 2d ed., II, chapter I, 211.

19. Adam Müller, *Friedrich II*, 305.

20. In addition to the well-known accounts of the Sand case, the following account relies in particular on the information provided by Wilhelm Hausenstein in the *Forschungen zur Geschichte Bayerns* XV (1907), 160, 224. Herr Dr. Hausenstein was also

kind enough to place at my disposal the comprehensive and valuable material that he has collected for a biography of Sand. The biography of Karl Follen, which appeared in a *Yearbook of the German-American Society* of Illinois for 1916, was not available to me.

21. André Suarès, *La nation contre la race*, II. *République et barbares* (Paris, 1917), 97. The well-known antitheses Orient-Occident, quantity-quality, and so on recur in much the same way, with motifs from the Apocalypse and world history, as was the case among anti-Napoleon romantics during the Napoleonic Wars. For the rest, I certainly would not want to define Suarès — the author of the fine essay on Dostoevsky — as a romantic. On the contrary, he has correctly noted that when Stendhal uses the word *romantic*, he does not mean it romantically at all. He means: Shakespeare and not Victor Hugo, Dante and not Chateaubriand, Beethoven and not Berlioz. Suarès adds, "A hundred years later, the ambiguity still exists. Political frauds cultivate it."

22. See Harnack, *Haucks Realenzyklopädie für protestantische Theologie*, 9, 614.

23. O. Gruppe, *Griechische Mythologie und Religionsgeschichte*, II (Munich, 1906), 1669. Gruppe notes that Frederick II and Voltaire "correctly recognized Julian as one of their own" (1663*n*. 2). This conforms to the view of all the Enlightenment figures of the eighteenth century. The marquis d'Argens, the friend of Frederick II, also explains and justifies the religious policy of Julian as a consequence of the intolerance of Christianity. See *Refléxions sur l'empereur Julian, vor der Ausgabe der Defénse du pagenisme*, 2n ed., I (Berlin, 1767), LXXXVI.

24. G. Negri, *L'imperatore Giuliano l'Apotata* (Milan, 1901), 491.

25. See Epistle 13 in J.C. Wolf, *Libanii Sophistae Epistolarum Centuria* (1711), 50. For further examples, see Wilmer Cave France, *The Emperor Julian's Relation to the New Sophistic and Neo-Platonism* (London, 1896), 20.

Index

and Gentz, 23, 134
and German romanticism, 57
individualism of, 64
on life vs. philosophy, 112
and Müller, 133–134, 135
and Schelling, 75, 112
and Schlegel, 89, 112, 114, 131
superlatives used by, 137
Finkenstein, 133
Frank, Hans, xi
Frederick II (king of Prussia), 102, 125, 155
French Revolution, 28–29
  arguments against, 109–110
  counterrevolutionary view of, 8
  and French royalists, 155
  German response to, 35–36, 41, 110–111, 112, 114
  Müller against, 40, 122–123
  opposition to, 122–123
  as pagan, 154
  partisans and enemies of as romantics, xxv
  revolutionaries' view of, 24
  Schlegel on, 36, 41–42, 130
  as symbol, 138
  Taine on, 12
Friedrich Wilhelm IV (king of Prussia), 149, 154

Gentz, Friedrich von, 22–23
  and Burke, 109, 130
  and 18th century, 63
  and Fichte, 23, 133–134
  and French Revolution, 122
  letters to, 75, 120
  and Metternich, 22, 23, 37
  and Müller, 23, 37, 39, 40, 42, 43, 46–48, 128, 133–134, 135, 143
  rhetorical talent of, 133
  and Schlegel, 23, 38, 118
  and Vienna Court, 37
Geulincx, Arnold, 85, 86, 98, 106
Gierke, Otto von, 17
Gneisenau, August von, 27
God
  collapse of traditional idea of, xix–xx, xxxi, 18, 58–59, 82, 91
  individual as tool of, 81
  in legitimist theories, 116
  monarch as corresponding to, 60
  for mystics, 67
  in occasionalism, 17, 82, 85, 94, 95, 99, 106, 122
Goering, Hermann, xi

Goethe, Johann Wolfgang von, 4, 23, 57, 66
  and Burke, 131
  escape by, 71
  and Müller, 41
  Novalis on, 83
  reaction against, 36
  and Schlegel, 131
  status of, 130
Görres, Johann Joseph von, 31, 49, 120, 135, 142
Gotzen, Count von, 44
Grimm, Wilhelm, 47, 145
Gruppe, Otto, 155, 157
Gutzkow, Karl Ferdinand, 130
Guyon, Madame, 54, 57

Haller, Carl Ludwig, 31–32, 153
  and Bonald, 114
  and Müller, 28, 49, 127
  Schlegel and Müller repeat, 125
  and state, 127, 138, 141–142
  and states of consent and rejection, 101, 102
Hamann, Johann Georg, 57
Hardenberg, Karl August von, 44–46
Hardouin, Father, 96
Harnack, Adolf von, 150
Haym, Rudolf, 22
Haza, 42
Hebert, 59
Hegel, G. W. F., 54, 64
  and ego-superego relation, 82
  and individual's relation to reason, 79–80
  and irony, 73
  new spirit from, 112
  and organism, 55
  on Rousseau, 111
  and Schelling, 112
  and Schlegel's theory, 113
  as South German, 32
Hegelianism, 24–25
  and "cunning of reason," 92
  and romanticism, 92, 151
Hemsterhuis, Francois (Frans), 57
Herder, Johann Gottfried von, 57, 58, 118
History
  as conservative demiurge, 60–64, 82
  as fanciful construction, 74–75
  individual as tool of, 81
  and occasionalism, 121–122
  romanticizing of, 69
Hobbes,Thomas, 54, 56
Hölderlin, Friedrich, 111

Irony and the Political Romantic
72: paralyzes the present

Self-centered Pol. Rom.
74: link to Writing Culture